A Reason for Hope

Natalie Cravens

always have hope!

-Natalie
Cravens

CreateSpace Publishing

ISBN: 1978210256
ISBN-13: 978-1978210257

A Reason for Hope
By Natalie Cravens

Acknowledgements go to St. Jude Children's Research Hospital and all of the doctors and nurses in A Clinic. Thank you for taking the absolute best care of me. I will forever be grateful for you and this amazing place.

Thank you to all of my family and friends for the love and support you gave me throughout this journey. I was continuously wrapped in comfort and prayers and I could never thank you enough. My family and I are especially thankful for Mardecia Sutton. Thank you for being such an incredible lifeline with every visit to and from Memphis. Your friendship is truly cherished.

Specially thanks to Richard England and Hunter Gunnels. Thank you Richard for planting the seed to write this book. You believed in me and never let me lose sight that my story should be told. Thank you Hunter for designing the perfect cover. You took a vison and brought it to life.

This book is in memory of Mallerie Graves, Mary Kate Rushing, Heather Braswell, and Regan Richards. I am thankful to have these angels watching over me. This book was written with precious memories and friendships that I hold dearly.

Chapter 1

The Unknown

My dad was in Nashville, Nicole, my twin sister was at soccer practice and James, my brother, was in the back yard working on one of his projects. My mom and I were the only ones in the house when the doctor's office called. She just kept saying, "ok" over and over again. I looked at my mom and waited for her to give me some kind of expression. Holding my breath just waiting for something, anything, but nothing, just a blank, cold, empty stare that said all the wrong things.

She looked at me with tears in her eyes and said, "You have Hodgkin's Lymphoma Cancer." Cancer. The only word that stuck in my head. I felt my heart drop because it instantly became heavy. I had no idea what Hodgkin's was, I just knew that it was cancer and to me that meant dying in a very slow way. This is how the story begins? Yes, on a beautiful day without a warning, without permission, without a care if it wrecks your life. That is cancer.

As my mom and I cried, all she could say was it was going to be all right, and we were going to get through this. Everything is going to be fine? We were going to get through this? How could I hear that when someone just told her I have cancer? What did "this" even mean? What was next, my date of death going to be discussed over the phone as well? My heart hurt, eyes burned, and my knees felt like they could give out at any moment. All I could hear was cancer. That word echoed in my head, and everything else was silent.

Things seemed to move in slow motion. What was I even supposed to do now? Should I call anyone? What do you even say to anyone? All mom and I were told was that I have cancer, and I needed to come back to the doctor's office tomorrow. Was it so hard to give me a few more answers? I needed answers to questions I did not even realize I had yet. I needed a manual for "Oh, you just found out you have cancer, here is what do you next", because I had no idea.

My mom went to the backyard to talk to my brother to let him know that the doctor had called. I walked to my room and started cleaning. My room all the sudden seemed cluttered, clothes were everywhere, and it bothered me. I picked shirts up off the floor, folded them, and put them away. My room looked better, but the palms of my hands now had a new job of collecting my tears. I stood in my dark room; face buried in my hands and cried alone. I just needed a minute. I needed everything to freeze, to let me catch up. I needed something, not someone. I needed a moment of nothing.

I made my way out the front door and sat on the steps of the porch. I wasn't comfortable, and I didn't know why I decided to sit there, but it seemed right. I've come to the conclusion bad news makes you do weird things. James sat down beside me with his arms around me as we both just cried. I love you was the only thing that was said, and that was perfect, maybe that was my moment of nothing. Words hurt and tried to make it better, but they couldn't; nothing could. His tears helped because it showed that it hurt someone else too. I didn't want anyone else to hurt from this, but I didn't want to be alone in the hurting either.

The silence was over. My dad was on the phone and wanted to talk. What was there to talk about? I had cancer, what else could be said? My dad told me that we would do everything possible to get me better, and we would all get through this together. He came through it with his cancer, and I can do it with mine too, is what he told me. How did my dad know we would get through my cancer? Knowing he was healthy and cancer free was great, but, nobody promised me that I would be as lucky. That only thing staring back at me was the reality that people die from cancer. Death wasn't on my list of things to do just yet, but sometimes we aren't given a choice.

As others began to find out, there were many hugs and words of "I love you." Everyone was sad, and I knew the news was shocking, but how do you think I felt? By now I was repeating, "Everything is going to be OK." If I was the one telling everyone it was going to be okay, what was everything telling me to make it okay? I'm so sorry, a hug, I'm praying for you, keep a positive attitude, all of those things are the words I heard. Yes, all of those things were nice, but all of it was just a reminder that I was now dying a little faster than the people around me, and everyone else was living a happy life just praying for me. I just wanted to look at them and say save it; I honestly don't care. I thought telling the people I loved would be the hardest thing to do, but it wasn't. Looking in the mirror was. When I saw my reflection all I would feel, hear, and taste was a monster inside me marking its calendar down, as to when to scare me, hurt me, and convince me I can't do this. Cancer hadn't even begun, and the reflection I saw had no control over what was going inside me. I saw people's concern, heard their prayers, and felt their love and support, but I was bitter and scared. That was okay, right?

I don't remember sleeping that night at all, but rather just laying in my bed thinking and looking at the ceiling. The next day at school was very hard, and facing everyone was the last thing I wanted to do. Everyone wanted to know, everyone wanted to talk, everyone wanted to be comforted. I just wanted to have five minutes without my heart hurting or tasting the same tears that seemed to never stop. I knew that a lot of people had heard about my diagnosis because I live in small town, but it was the thought of starting off the day by retelling things over and over again that made me feel sick to my stomach. Walking down the halls seemed to cause an awkward silence as some people looked with curiosity while others shared a sad look. Seeing many people sad and crying was a little scary. Why were they so upset? Was there something they knew that I wasn't aware of yet? I mean I wasn't dead, but the way some were acting I was already at the funeral home, flowers picked out, and people were bracing themselves to put in me the ground.

Spending my day at school crying wasn't my idea, but I did choose to go. Throughout the day, it felt like things were in a daze, and classes seemed to go by very slowly. Concentrating in class was difficult, and school was in the back of my mind. My drama teacher led a prayer for me during class. He thought it would be important to turn to the only thing that would truly hold my hand and get me through the day. While everyone wanted to talk or ask questions, he suggested a prayer. That was the only form of comfort that I found throughout that vast building filled with great people. That moment I felt God at work.

Later that day, I was checked out of school because I had an appointment with the doctor that did my surgery. He wanted to talk to my parents and me about what would happen in the future and our options. We got to the doctor's office and sat down until my name was called. While I kept moving in my chair, I wondered if the girl across from me had gotten cancer news too, probably not though. I flipped through a magazine until my name was called and then the nurse led us to the room. The doctor showed sympathy, but not like what I wanted. He was the one who saw and touched the cancerous lymph nodes, and I wanted him to be sad. Angry. Anything! He took them out, and gave me bad news, and all he could do was say he was sorry! I wondered what he felt when he was doing my surgery and knew it was cancer. Did he feel sorry, or think how hard it would be for me? Maybe, maybe not, but this sucked. I was in a room talking about options to the man that saw the monster inside me. I was cold and scared while we just discussed stupid options. The surgeon said that I could receive treatment in Jackson or if we had thought of another place. We had talked the night before about St. Jude Children's Research Hospital. This was all happening too fast. We could have picked from a hat for all I cared.

However, I did know this was a more serious decision than I was making it out to be. St. Jude was the place I did not want to be but needed to be. It was for kids and teens with cancer, I appropriately fell into that category and knew that had to be the place.

In anger, sadness, and exhaustion I knew there was hope. It was something that was hard to feel, far out of my reach, but I was, at least, giving it credit for being present somewhere in me. The hope I was holding onto wasn't big enough yet to allow myself to be completely consumed in it though.

Chapter 2

The Road Ahead

I have always had a great group of friends. Some of us were closer than others, but I had a pretty large group of friends. One night, 12 of my friends decided to stop by and see me. It was good to have them there, but there wasn't much to say. It is okay not to know what to say. I didn't know what to say. They were all showing me support in the way they knew how, and that was just by surrounding me. Was there a feeling of being alone even in a house full of people that cared? Yes, but for a small period of time, the house that had been filled with tears was now full of laughter. I couldn't let that feeling take over the act of my friends doing something good. Though feeling alone, I enjoyed hearing laughter and the familiarity of a night with friends. That was nice.

Church was the next day, and that was going to be another set of people to deal with. It was a regular Sunday, except for the cancer part, everyone was trying to get a hot shower, get ready, and make it out the door early enough to make it to Bible class. We did have time to take a quick picture of the whole family. It was weird though, why did we even take a picture? It was like I was going to disappear soon, so we had to take a picture. The picture wasn't a big deal, but it's weird how something that changes in life can make you do again, weird things. What if that was the last picture we would all take? It wasn't, and I knew it probably wouldn't be, but what was the purpose? Maybe to think, oh, that was the family cancer picture. Everyone looked nice, with a frozen smile. Strangers would never be able to tell the feelings everyone had in the photo, but every time I would see it, those feelings would always be there.

On the way to church, I let everyone know that this wasn't going to be a cry-fest. I knew people would want to hug, ask questions, and talk to me. I entertained the thought of having my own service between God and me, but that only remained an idea. My name was put on the prayer list. It sent goose bumps down my spine hearing the prayers. I couldn't escape the sadness anywhere! Even in the prayers, voices were shaky, and some of the men I could tell were holding back tears. I just wanted to worship. That's all! Was it so hard to take a time and let me breathe and just hear the worshiping around me? Yes, the prayers were great, and I know God was listening, but I was exhausted.

People would place their hand on my back and tell me a story of someone they knew that had had the same thing, and they were doing great now. That's great…really it is, but that has to be on the top list of things not to tell someone who has just met cancer. I hadn't even begun fighting against this disease, and people were telling me things about it. I wanted to cry, really cry, the kind where you can't breathe because all your energy is in your tears.

Church, talking, and hugging ended and I went to the place where I felt safe…home. I didn't have to fake smile, hug anyone, and I could roll my eyes at a positive attitude if I heard one. I could also just be with people that let me be sad, or talk about anything else but cancer.   Dad got the call that St. Jude wanted me there at 9:00 A.M. Monday. Cold feet have sunk in, and I didn't want to go. I felt fine. I didn't want to pack, and I didn't want to stay in a hospital. Thanks dad for making the call, but no thanks.

Seriously, what do you even take to a cancer hospital? Can I take my own pillow, or do I have to have to use a germ-free plastic wrapped one? Can I take my iPod to block out the annoying doctors that will ask a million questions? I didn't know what to take. Mom told me to take whatever made me comfortable. Okay, that sounds good, so the next question was who was driving the U-Haul to take my whole room to St. Jude? Mom knew I didn't want to go, but she just kept saying it was an answered prayer to get into St. Jude. Perhaps it was, but I didn't even pray for cancer, and somehow my life answered to that.

I sat on my bedroom floor with my books and backpack on one side of me and a suitcase on the other. It was like my past was on one side, and the future was on the other. The suitcase was there, and my past wouldn't fit in the suitcase, and all I could take were things to make my future a little more comfortable. My response every time I was asked how packing was coming was that it sucked and I wasn't going, I wasn't packing, and I was going to school instead. Nicole wanted me to stay, and we wanted to team up against this, like everything else in our lives, but we couldn't. I was alone in this and still had an empty suitcase.

I could think of a lot of terrible people in the word that deserved this more than me so why the hell did I get picked? I would never wish cancer on anyone, but why a 17-year-old girl that was enjoying life made decent grades, obeyed her parents for the most part, and overall really was a good person? Everyone says God has a plan and things happen for a reason, but I can't think of one solid reason cancer was a plan for me. I couldn't trust anyone when they said things would be okay or work out. What if they didn't work out? Explain that to my twin that doesn't understand any of this either. My dad would hold me and tell me that he loved me. That warmed my heart. It didn't take the pain away, but it stopped it for a few minutes. Being in his arms felt safe, like, this cancer couldn't hurt me. I could tell that it was hurting my dad. It hurt, a pain that stabs you in the heart, seeing your parents hurt for you and all you can do it watch.

I didn't have to set an alarm or wait for my mom to wake me up. It didn't seem like I was getting up early because I never had fallen asleep. I got up, got ready, and didn't say much. James and I let the hug we shared do more of the talking than actual words. A hug that had fear and hope wrapped all around it. A hug that said I can't take this away, but I would if it were possible. That was the feeling I packed with me.

Nicole woke up, and before she even made it half way down the hall and out to the living room to see me, she was crying. We hugged for what felt like forever. I didn't want to let go. My go to person couldn't go with me. We needed each other, and I knew it was going to be a hard day for Nicole just as much as it was for me. She had to go to school without me and didn't know how long she would have to do that. I didn't want Nicole to have to drive to school and leave by herself. I wanted to be at school so we could laugh and make fun of each other. I didn't want Nicole to look over at my desk 5 out of 7 classes and be reminded that I wasn't returning anytime soon. I wanted to protect her; this was the biggest moment of sadness and fear we had ever experienced for each other. I needed God to get us through the day. I couldn't put words together to form a pray; I went off of knowing that he knew my heart and what I was asking.

It was just me, my parents, and the open road to St. Jude. Now, it seemed early. We passed several cars, and I saw people talking on their phones, driving kids to school, going to work, just living their lives. No matter how much we want life to stop, hold on, or give us a minute, it doesn't. People keep living, and days continue to pass.

In between dozing off I wondered what things would be like if we could look at other people and just know their pain. Would everyone be more willing to help others out, or would we all continue living and worrying about our individual struggles? Maybe people would be more understanding, or maybe it would cause more pain for people. I didn't know, but I still wanted people to know what was happening in my life. Not for attention, but rather as a reminder to enjoy the days where pain and struggles aren't the main things going on.

The buildings were light pink and nothing like I pictured. You can tell yourself you are ready, I can do this, and then the elevator opens, and you freeze. You see parents, kids, wagons, blankets, IV polls, lab coats, huge red binders being pushed around on carts, and sickness. Overlooking painted walls and baldheads is

15

impossible. The sterile hospital smell has seeped into your pores and all you can do stare. A lady broke my stare and asked if she could help us. My parents told her we had an appointment, and we were new. She took my name and then asked us to be seated until we were called back to the room. We sat against a wall that faced all the patients walking in the open area. Kids were getting sheets of paper, purple bracelets, and finding places to sit. Everything was a waiting game; everyone seemed so familiar with everything. You could hear patient's names being said over the intercom telling them what clinic to go to, or if it was their time for treatment in the medicine room. This was a regular thing for them, and I couldn't wrap my head around it.

All the walls were painted, and I'm sure that helps the little kids, but those paintings weren't fooling me. The only slightest cool thing that caught my eye was the girl that looked the same age as me with a lime green and hot pink Mohawk. I loved the Mohawk, but dad seemed to think otherwise by the way his eyes bugged out when he saw it. I cracked a smile that seemed unfamiliar, but it was nice. I still wasn't convinced about this place just yet, but I was giving it a shot. I honestly had no other choice at this point. Everyone was so nice. These people loved their jobs and were just trying to make me as comfortable as possible. My bitterness covered up my sadness and shadowed my politeness some, so I decided to give these people a break. They wanted to help, not hurt me, and they weren't the ones to give me cancer; it just happened.

The nurses were only able to get half of the vials the lab needed for blood work because they had to stick me so many times.

I learned I have small veins that roll…who knew? The other half of my blood work would get done when I got my PICC line put in. Now they were talking a different language. PICC line? I sure was hoping that was a line you got in to pick when you get to leave, but for some reason, I don't think that was their discussion.

We were shown around to different parts of the hospital by a couple of different nurses and then they took us to A Clinic. I learned where I would always sign in at and then wait to see my Doctor. I was already lost in this huge place with people I didn't know and words I didn't understand. We met and talked with all the people in A Clinic, which is the Leukemia and Lymphoma Clinic. This is where I would see my doctor every visit to St. Jude. I was asked medical history questions and about recent doctors visits. My parents were the ones to ask all the doctors the questions because I had no idea where to start. I did want to know when I would lose my hair and if I was going to die. All the other stuff could wait, but if I was going to die or lose my hair we had to start planning and figuring out some major things in my book.

The first day, as well as the whole week, was the most overwhelming thing. A couple of people told us that you could always tell who the new families are because they have that glazed look in their eyes. I thought it was the having hair part that gave it away though. Dad had to leave to get back to Nicole and James during the week. It was just going to be mom and me. No matter who was there I still had cancer, but I wanted my mom there. She had calmness about her during such a stressful time that made me feel at ease. That is what made me feel at home in a place that wasn't my home at all.

Chapter 3

Ready or Not

That week we stayed at the Grizzle House at St. Jude. Patients who were having short visits or that were new stayed in that building. Volunteer's came and brought activities for everyone. I always looked for someone my age, but it always seemed to be younger kids. Being around the kids and other people helped since it had been a long week.

I sat with a girl named Melody, who was a few years younger than me. She was from another country and has been coming to St. Jude for six years. She was only here for a check up but had to stay a year and a half the first time she came to St. Jude. A year and a half because of being sick, I just couldn't wrap my head around that. We finished our conversation with Melody and her mom and then headed to the room. It was nice talking to another person close to my age, but I wanted to have at least someone to talk to that completely understood what I was going through that week, and the weeks ahead.

Scans were the next day, and I even got to listen to music. The two scans lasted awhile, but they were peaceful in a weird way. No one was asking me anything, and all I could hear was my music. I enjoyed the quiet, and for the first time in a week, I escaped from it all. Maybe God was calming my nerves and listening to all the prayers. After finishing with the scans, I was done with things for the day. I was a free girl! Friends and family had stopped by to see me. I enjoyed seeing everyone, and it was nice to laugh for a little while. I didn't like the situation I was in, but that didn't make me lose my love for laughing.

Everyone always wanted to know how I was doing so before we ever left for St. Jude mom set me up a web page that we updated daily to let everyone know what was going on day to day. Phone calls, text, and emails were nice to get, but it was a huge help to update the page and have people read that and leave me comments on there. It was always easy to sound like everything was fine in text messages or emails because if I didn't make things seem okay, they wouldn't understand why. If I made the procedures sound easy or that I was feeling positive, then no one had to worry about it. I was positive as much as I could, but mom knew. She knew everything I was feeling wasn't positive, but she tried to keep the situation positive for me.

I hadn't been at St. Jude long and I already noticed I kept walking the same halls, saying the same patient number, seeing the same doctors, and hearing the same thing, but I couldn't remember any of it. I probably wasn't trying to remember any of the important things, but who could blame me? Everyone kept talking about medical stuff to me, but I never saw anything being done about the cancer. Wasn't that the whole reason I was there? I understand there is a lot to go on with cancer, but I was ready to get on with it. Everything kept building, and I hadn't cried in front of anyone at the hospital. Walking through the halls, I felt like I had to suck it up.

These kids weren't crying so that meant I shouldn't. I was tired of that. If God had a plan and was taking care of me, why was I still scared and worried. I trusted in him, but so much was happening that the trust I had was getting pushed farther and farther away.

St. Jude was just a place I saw on TV when the program about the hospital came on, and not a place I would end up. I had watched the programs about St. Jude many times and hated to see the suffering many kids have to go through, and now I was one of those kids. The money donated was now helping me. I don't live that far from Memphis yet when I would see the shows it seemed like a place so far away. Now that I'm here, I know it is close to my home yet another world, a world of not just any cancer, but childhood cancer, sickness, medicines, pain, loss, but hope, love, and courage. I saw the hope and courage in others, but did they walk in the door with that? Did someone tell the people how to have it, or did you have to find it all on your own? I had it, but was it just pretend? I wanted to have the hope and courage like everyone else seem to have. Life before illness now appeared to focus on the things that weren't very important. All of the sudden clinging to that hope and relying on my faith was something I was searching for in my days.

Dr. Howard met with us to go over chemo treatments. I would be getting treatments every other week for five months. I didn't ask questions because I didn't know what to ask. Chemo to me was going to be poison to make me feel better somehow. Later that day I was scheduled to have my PICC line put in. Kelly, the Child Life Specialist at St. Jude was going to be able to stay with me the whole time. I didn't know what a PICC line was. The doctors explained it to me that it was a tube they would put in one of my main veins in my arm. They would feed the tube through my arm, and it would end close to my heart. This procedure was how I would receive chemo and get my blood work done instead of trying to get an IV.

Kim, the lady putting my line in told me everything she was doing because I couldn't see what was going on. I could feel the pressure of the tube they were weaving through my arm. Kelly had a hold of one of my hands while a nurse had a hold of my other hand. Holding on to their hands was comforting, but I knew God was there with me as well. He was telling me to hang in there and I was, but it wasn't the easiest thing to do. Kelly even mentioned I wasn't squeezing their hands hard enough. As bad as it hurt and as much as I wanted to squeeze their hands extra hard I couldn't. I was motionless with tears streaming down my face as I stared at a certain ceiling tile that was painted with kids on it. It kept my attention focused on thinking about all the other children that had been right there in the exact spot. How could something so awful as cancer even begin to touch kids? It didn't make any sense.

Kelly fizzled out my thoughts by asking if I was okay, and all I could do was nod. She stood there the whole time and caught every single tear before they ran down into my ears. After two tries of unsuccessfully getting my PICC line in they decided it would be better to put me to sleep the next day and try again. It was such a relief to know that I was going to be asleep instead of awake again. I never wanted to have to do that again. Everyone apologized because this was supposed to be a simple procedure.

I was done for the day, and I knew Nicole and a close friend Cliff were on their way to Memphis. Our laughter that night erased the eventful day. I couldn't remember the last time I laughed that hard. We all put hats on and tucked in our hair. Was it too soon to joke about that stuff? I'm not sure, but it was healing. Laughter and being with people I love truly were the best medicine.

The next day everything was ready for the putting of the PICC line in again. Kelly was there, and I heard the same stuff as the day before. I tried not to worry, but things were completely out of my control, everything was. The next thing I knew I was waking up in recovery barely able to hold my head up from all the drugs. My sister and mom got a good laugh at me after surgery. The day wasn't over, and we still had to meet with Radiology, the line nurse and pick up supplies for my mom to flush my PICC line, and get my first chemo treatment. Mom would have to flush my line every day to keep it working. The Line Nurse was going to teach my mom how to flush the line, and keep it clean from infection. All of this information was overwhelming to me; I could only imagine how it made my mom feel. Along with having cancer I now have this thing sticking out of my arm that looked like a little extra arm. It looked weird to say the least. We kept it wrapped against my arm for protection, and that was good because I didn't want to see it.

It was now chemo time for this girl. My best friend Kayla brought her mom and some friends to my first treatment. I was shocked to see them. It made me nervous to share my treatment with them. I didn't know what to expect so I couldn't exactly explain it to them. It wasn't easy letting more friends into all the details of cancer. I didn't know how to introduce them to something that is so cruel. I felt sick, and my best friend was there to see me. I wanted to be the same person that always had fun not that was always sick. I couldn't be both all the time. It was hard and confusing. She didn't care; she just wanted to be there. To know where I was, see me, look at each other and know it's been a long week and not even have to talk about it. That was a break I needed.

Before leaving, we were greeted by a lady with the brightest smile. We hadn't met this lady before, but she introduced herself and said her name was Mardecia. She lived in Memphis, and wanted to let us know that if we needed anything she would be there. She volunteered at the hospital, and just within those few minutes, I knew how big of a blessing she truly was to families there.

Chapter 4

Nothing Routine

Kayla spent the night, and we didn't do anything special we just spent time together like always. Kayla was worried about me, and I worried about her, but we didn't talk about it. We went to bed early knowing we all would be going back home together the next day.

I woke up feeling surprisingly good. Everyone had told me the day after chemo would be terrible, but I felt fine. I was tired and didn't feel the best, but it wasn't any worse than normal. I was confused. I could handle chemo if I was going to still feel okay. We packed the car and mom, Kayla, and I were on our way home! The place I felt safe and enjoyed being. The warmth I felt when just lying on the couch with my favorite blanket and pillow. That was what I was the reason I was excited.

We got in the door, and all I wanted to do was sit and soak up the fact that I was in a familiar place. I walked in my room, and my eyes lit up. I had two huge signs hanging on my walls. One said, "We Love You" and the other one said " We Miss You," everyone at school had signed it with a note or just their name. That made me so happy. I stood there not knowing where to begin reading what people had written but, once I started reading them, I couldn't stop until I had read every single one. They all made me smile, and some even made me laugh. By the time, I was done reading them I had tears running down my face because it made me feel good to know so many people had been thinking about me.

After that, I laid down because I was starting to feel sick from treatment. Kayla stayed the rest of the day, and I wasn't very good company that afternoon. I started feeling worse, and quickly realized this was just the beginning. Kayla and Nicole both now realized how sick I was going to start being. It made mom nervous to think how many germs I would be around with people visiting. Kayla took a piece of paper, marker, and a bottle of hand sanitizer outside. She posted a sign that said "you must sanitize your germs before entering", and made sure everyone sanitized. Mom was relieved; but I smelled the hospital at my own house. I guess it was nice everyone was trying to keep me healthy.

The next few days after treatment I still didn't feel well. Each morning mom would wake me up to take my daily pills. Maybe a few pills would have been okay, but I think they sent the whole pharmacy home with me! I felt fine until chemo started and now I was taking more than I ever had. These doctors had it all wrong I think. Medicine was supposed to make you feel better, not like you were going to throw up every minute. I was nauseous, tired, achy, bones hurt, and my insides hurt from the inside out.

In the midst of all of this, I remembered that I still had school. I probably even had homework due, but I couldn't remember. What was I going to do about school? I had to pass, but there was no way I could go to school like this. Right when I kept asking mom about school and flooded her with all of these how's, what ifs, and whens she knew I was getting overwhelmed and upset. She had me lay down and said not to worry about it. School needed to be the least of my worries at the moment. I needed everyone to understand though that I had to stay on track; I wanted to graduate the next year. I knew mom would work things out, but it still overwhelmed me. She made some phone calls, and after everything was worked out, she told me I would have a homebound teacher come to the house. The teacher was my math teacher, Mrs. Maxwell. The homebound school didn't sound so bad when I had one of my favorite teachers helping me. My principal said I could go to school when I felt like it, but I would do my work with Mrs. Maxwell. This put my mind at ease. If I had a hard time showering and doing daily activities due to lack of energy, how would I ever walk the halls, study, and keep up the pace with everyone like this? Why did everything have to be so difficult now?

Mom offered to help me take a shower and thought that might help me feel better. Since I had been home, I had slept a lot and just taken a bath because I couldn't get my PICC line wet. We had to figure something out because I did not want to continue taking baths. Mom bought Press & Seal wrap and decided to wrap my whole upper arm and tape it. I couldn't move my arm, but there was no water getting close to that PICC! Whoever came up with this idea and told mom about it was a genius! This was a vital thing to have in my day if I was showering. Who knew that simple tasks would become so difficult? My energy was used to take a shower...just one simple shower! Seriously, how embarrassing is that? Have your mom wrap your arm and make sure you didn't pass out. Every 17-year-old dreams of that, right?

I had treatments every other week and after this first week of my treatment, I felt dreadful, and right when I started feeling better again I had to go back for another treatment. We decided that mom would stay home with me for the week after my first treatment, but then when I got to the point where I was doing better I could stay at home by myself. There wasn't anything anyone could do so why just stand around; I didn't mind staying by myself either. Mom's work was close by, and I could always call if I needed her or anyone else. I could handle time alone just fine. I had cancer I wasn't a baby. I had a couch, TV, Internet, books, food everyone kept bringing by, and a phone; this girl would be just fine. Convincing everyone else that I would be okay wasn't the easiest thing to do though.

It was time for my second treatment, and everything had gone fine as far as I knew from the last one. Besides feeling awful from the treatment, I didn't know what to expect. My grandparents were going with us, this time, to see what St. Jude was like. I was just going to be there two days, so that was better than a week.

Every treatment visit starts on a Sunday night with blood work and Chemo and doctor visit on Monday. This set up made things a lot easier on treatment day. It helps to get that stuff out of the way; it also saves time and energy because Mondays are usually busy at the hospital.

We checked into Grizzly House and then walked over to the hospital. I got my patient bracelet and got checked in to get blood work done. Blood work now doesn't take long at all because of my PICC line. This visit to triage was different than the last time they used my PICC line, though. The nurse had trouble getting all the blood needed and thought that my line might be in an odd position. We were all hoping that was the case. She flushed my line with no problem and said everything looked good as far as she could tell. Flushing the line was honestly the worst part of it. Although I never have to swallow anything I can taste the Saline solution once it is pushed through my line. The only way I can think to describe it is an awful metal, chemical, sterile liquid that tastes so bad it can make you ears burn and gag reflexes go to work. It only takes a second, but those few seconds sure are terrible.

Nicole decided to come with all of us too because we were meeting dad in Memphis on his way home from being out of town that weekend. We all went to eat and enjoyed being together. The night was still early, but knowing it was going to be a busy day when we got up in the morning we decided to head back to St. Jude. We showed my grandparents around the Grizzly House and then went up to the room. I was glad my grandparents decided to come. It wasn't my first pick of a place to hang out with my family, but they wanted to see what my new environment was like.

Later that night while changing I noticed my left arm had a purple color to it, and it seemed like it was swollen. I looked at it for a few minutes and thought it is probably nothing, but worriedly I yelled for my mom to look at it. I hadn't noticed anything strange about how I was feeling and since I'd never been through this before I didn't have anything to compare to what was normal. We didn't know what to do but had been told if anything was ever wrong to go to the hospital and a doctor could see me. We didn't know if it was serious or not; maybe we were just overreacting? However, we woke up my grandparents to let them know then mom and I headed to the hospital. The medicine room, which is where I receive treatment, stays open throughout the night with a doctor on call. We got to the medicine room and saw the doctor. He measured my arms, and my left arm was definitely swollen. There wasn't anything he could do right then but said he ordered an ultrasound for me the next morning. I would be okay to on back to bed for the night, so we finished talking to the doctor and headed back hopefully for the rest of the evening.

The next day was going to be busy, and of course, I couldn't sleep. I was worried about my arm. What was causing all of this? What about my PICC line? I said a prayer for God to calm my nerves but still was worried. Why can't it be easy? Just tell myself to stop, or to put complete trust in God to calm everything? It didn't seem like God was trying to take my worries away. I really felt like I was trying, but getting nowhere.

Before I knew it, my mom was telling me that I needed to get up and get ready. Didn't I just go to bed, though? This time, that routine I talked about earlier then one I wouldn't get the hang of now was very easy. Mom gave Justine the list of supplies and medicines I would need for the next two weeks while Dr. Howard measured my arm. He said I would have an ultrasound on my arm, and then they would look at it and see if there was a blood clot in my line. Dr. Howard had told me that no matter what I was having chemo before the day was over. I was fine without that awful stuff, though. Off to the ultrasound mom and I went while my grandparents waited in the waiting room. Ultrasound didn't take long and then it was another waiting game.

Chapter 5

Hidden Dangers

I was beginning to feel exhausted. It usually didn't take long, but when you're anxious to hear news, you become physically and mentally tired. We were called back to the exam room where Dr. Howard met us. He said I have a blood clot in my arm and that my PICC line needed to come out. He scheduled it to be removed the next day and told us they would put me to sleep to do it. Before I could even say no, the whole next day was planned and explaining everything that would happen. He said if they were not able to dissolve the entire clot after taking out my PICC line I would be put on TPA, which is a high powered blood thinner and monitored in the ICU. The TPA drug would just be used if there were one or more blood clots. I wasn't too excited about any of this, and there was still Chemo waiting for me too.

Grandma placed her arm around me while I waited to have chemo. I thought this was supposed to be a quick visit? Could my body just not go along with this plan for the next few months? I was going along with thing whether I wanted to or not, so I thought it was time for my body to do the same. I sat and watched the little kids around me. I think about all the little kids that are going through such harsh treatments, and some of the kids are so little that they won't even remember it and others the treatments will affect them the rest of their lives. Some run around like nothing is wrong and don't even realize they are sick while you see others laying down in a wagon so sick they can't hold their heads up. It breaks my heart to sit there and think how sick some of the kids are. They shouldn't have to go through this. It wasn't fair to anyone. The question why was still left unanswered. Maybe these questions would always be unanswered, though.

It was my second treatment so I felt like I knew what all would happen. The nurse always gets everything ready by putting on a gown and gloves. I have three chemo drugs that I get. I am first started on a medicine for nausea, and that only takes about 20 minutes. I remember at my first treatment seeing the chemo for the first time. It's just a liquid, but when they bring it to you in a Biohazard bag, and the nurses are dressed in their gowns and gloves you begin to think that they are putting that in you, and the aren't even allowed to touch it! That is crazy! You have to look at it and tell yourself that is what is going to make me better and not think about that huge biohazard sign on it. Things at my first treatment seemed so busy with everyone there and were so distracted that this time my full attention was on these drugs. These three chemicals that were red, lime green, and clear were the drugs that would save my life, but make me feel like I'm dying.

We headed to the car and started home. I was ready to get home because I didn't feel well already, but then I would have to leave again to come right back to St. Jude. This time, after treatment, I started feeling sick faster than last time. Two treatments down at this point and I couldn't begin to imagine how I was going to make it through 6 more of these things. That didn't seem like a lot, but it felt like a million.

I could only lie down for a little while before I had to start packing again. James and Nicole welcomed me home when they got home, but I didn't seem to care. I wasn't staying, so it wasn't a welcome home. They were excited to see me, and I wanted to be excited back, but I wasn't. I wasn't happy, and I felt like I was green all over from the nausea feeling that had taken over my body. I later moved to my room to lie on my bed. I thought I might start packing, but then I saw my bed, and it just looked to great to pass up. I couldn't resist. Mom came back to check on me and just gave me a pitiful look. She could tell without even asking how I felt. Without missing a beat, mom started packing my things. Didn't ask me to help and knew what I wanted, but at this point, it didn't matter what was packed. When did all these terrible drugs start taking over my body? It felt like the sickness had been creeping up on me and then out of nowhere my body had been consumed by exhaustion and nausea. If I could throw up, I would probably feel fine, but I couldn't even do that. All I could do was lay motionless hoping it would go away.

We stopped at Subway on the way out of town. I didn't want to eat, and everything sounded gross. Subway was a little more crowded than what I would have liked, but I walked inside with mom. We saw people that asked how I was doing. I could feel the angry building as my throat starting burning and my breaths became short. I wanted to scream at them! Were they blind? My upper arm was wrapped so people wouldn't stare at my line, I was wearing pajamas, I looked like I hadn't slept, and my face felt like all the color at drained down to my toes. That was how I was doing. But the only thing that I said faintly was momma…as I started to lose my balance. It was time to leave, and I had to sit down. When I felt okay enough, we left. My emotions were crazy. My steroids made me nervous and could barely catch my breath. All of this resulted in crying half of the way to Memphis. What kind of strong person just cries all the time? The only answer I came up with was one that has cancer or that wasn't very strong. I was strong, and I let everyone know that, but no one would see my tears. My mom did, though, she didn't just see them she felt them and caught them as soon as they formed. My strength was in those tears and comfort was in my mom's hands. I realized that I kept trying to figure out how I was going to put this all behind me when needed to figure out how to get through it. Those weren't easy tasks, but they were important. I needed to try and work through this. I had a fire inside me to beat this thing, but I kept letting it out. I had to use the positivity from others to maybe try and keep it going when I didn't have the positivity from myself.

The morning came way too quickly but isn't that how it always tends to be with something you aren't looking forward to doing. I wasn't able to eat or drink anything because I was being put to sleep, but I was getting used to that because of all the tests I had gone through. The more I was at the hospital, the more it was familiar. It wasn't my favorite, but it wasn't a stranger. Dad came that morning, and the nurse led us to the operating room. Same hospital smell, same cold, uncomfortable bed, same people, and the same nurse. The nurse and doctors were still in the process of getting everything ready, but they could take as long as they needed. I sat on the bed while my parents seemed so far away. My dad tried so hard to hold his tears back, and mom looked at me with the most caring look. Those moments when I looked at them, my heart cried out in pain as if I was 6. Life was so serious now. The only expressions then were heartache and worry.

James called and wanted to talk before they started. My shaky voice made him aware of how nervous I was. He tried to make me laugh and crack a smile, but my head was so clouded with other things. As my mom leaned down and kissed my head, as my dad followed. Our eyes locked and my heart sunk further into my chest as they shut the door behind them. My head faced the ceiling as tears silently rolled out of the corner of my eyes. Everyone comforted me and gave me something for my nerves. Everything else faded away.

I woke up to being moved over to a hospital bed and nurses looking over me talking. I couldn't tell you what they were saying, but I do remember one nurse telling me that they found another blood clot, so they had to put me on TPA. This is just what Dr. Howard was hoping wouldn't happen. The doctor explained to my parents that once they got the first clot dissolved, they moved closer to the end of the PICC line and found another clot closer to my heart about the size of the end of his thumbnail. I would be on the TPA IV drip and then the next morning I would go in for a dye test to see if the clot had dissolved like it was supposed to. I wasn't aware of any of this, and I don't think I was even aware of who I was. I was transported to the ICU and only woke up off and on. I finally woke up and couldn't see my parents anywhere. That was such a scary feeling. The nurse saw I was awake and got them for me. They tried to explain everything, but I just kept zoning in and out. I slept the day away but was in pain all night. My whole body hurt. My chest hurt every time I took a breath; everything seemed to be getting worse. I was certain they had let a train run me over during the procedure.

When I got into ICU, I already had an IV in which helped a lot, because they were giving me medication through the IV they had used during the procedure. Unfortunately, that soon didn't work, and they had to put in another one. That night was horrible, and it seemed like it was never going to end. I had never experienced this much pain. It wasn't in one spot or just for a few minutes. It felt like my insides were being destroyed. This is the first time I really thought I might be sick enough to die. Seriously, if this was how cancer was, someone could kill me off now. Cancer was now the worst physical and emotional pain that had ever entered my life. I was given pain medication, but there wasn't enough to help. A low dose of sedation was used to help me rest and deal with the pain, but no one knew why things were going this way.

The next day was bearable. The dye test was going to be done to see if both of the clots had dissolved. We were told it was scheduled to be done sometime in the afternoon. Morning or afternoon I couldn't tell you what time of day it even was. I didn't know what to expect or how the test was going to be done. The nurse, my parents, and I all went together for them to do the scan. One of the nurses there started explaining to all of us what was about to go on. I had a blue catheter in my left arm where my PICC line was, and they would just put this dye through it and look at a screen that would show if they had been dissolved. She said it wouldn't hurt, and it shouldn't take that long.

My mom and dad left the room as I lay down on the table. The nurse got me a blanket because I was freezing and then the doctor walked over to the table and told me they were about to begin. The dye test started, and I was still shaking from between being cold and a little nervous. My thoughts were blank. I just looked at the same ceiling tile as all the times before. There wasn't anything to think about. My head hurt from thinking. It was painless, and the doctor said everything looked good, and the TPA had dissolved the clots. Knowing that made me happy because it gave me the hope that if all was ok, I would be able to go home! My parents got back up to the room with me, and my nurse told me that I would have to be there a little bit longer so they could monitor me without the tube in my arm. I could handle a little longer if I were at least getting to go home.

I wasn't excited to hear that I would have to have shots twice a day from then on out because of the blood clots. Shots? Really? Because chemo and medicine weren't enough for me. I was going to get to go home without a PICC line to flush for at least two weeks. Dr. Howard said that if all went well, I could go home and return the day before my next chemo treatment so they could put in another PICC line. No line? No problem! Mom wouldn't have to flush my line for a few days, and I would be able to shower without wrapping my arm! Sounded like a break to me.

Chapter 6

The Unexpected

My mom and nurse help me up because I had to use the bathroom and as soon as I stood up I couldn't hear anything, I saw black spots, and then everything went black. My blood pressure had dropped to 50/27, and that is dangerously low. I remember standing up and feeling weird, but I didn't think I was passing out. It was scary to lose your hearing and then feel your body just kind of crumble. My mind and body had gone to an entirely different place it seemed. It was a scary thing. I tried to convince my mom and nurse that I was just fine and to let me get back up. They thought otherwise and said I wasn't getting up and that I wasn't fine.

I was saying out loud I felt fine, and that things weren't that bad, but I didn't feel fine in any way. But saying it that way I thought could make it that way. When all the excitement happened, the nurse rushed to get dopamine, which brings your blood pressure up and your heart rate down. They decided to keep me on that a little while since my blood pressure was still running low. I knew things weren't looking good, but I wasn't sure I wanted to know what was happening to me. If I didn't ask questions, then I might be able to keep from worrying about more things. As the day went on, mom never left my side. Even if I was asleep, I could still feel her there.

The evening became stressful for me as my nurse came in and told me they had to find two new IV locations. I was being given so much medication that is was hard on my veins, and the other IV's were giving out. They had already had a hard time getting in the others, so they knew I was a hard stick. I was stuck in my hands, feet, and arms. Black and blue marks seemed to cover my hand and arms. I was started on three different IV antibiotics because of possible infection and IV fluids because my fluid level had begun to drop.

Things seemed to have gone from bad to worse in just a day. By now they had already started to take vials of blood and to do blood cultures to see what infections were forming. Not only was my heart rate and blood pressure affected but now my kidneys were barely functioning. Everything that was happening kept getting worse. I had no control over anything it seemed. I watched my monitor as much as I could, but I couldn't control my blood pressure or heart rate. I could only watch.

That night my mom was sitting next to me and asked if I wanted her to read me some of the things people had sent us online. I said yeah hoping that some of them would cheer me up. I always loved reading what people wrote me. Some of them made me laugh, others made me miss certain people, and all of them made me cry. Tears because lots of people were pulling for me and sad because I hated being like this. Mom had been posting on our blog, and she had updated this:

"My precious daughter is so strong and courageous just like the song, but it is so hard not to be afraid even when she knows God is with her each and every day. She never complains but goes through with the things needed in spite of her pain. I tell her I'm not sure I would be as brave as she is all the time. Today has had a wonderful blessing; God has answered the prayers of many that her blood clots would be dissolved." By this time, I had tears rolling down my cheeks, and my mom had to stop and ask if I wanted her to stop. I said, " No, I am fine. Keep reading".

"There is only one small area that wasn't cleared up, and that will probably be taken care of through injections she will be getting twice a day from her on out. The situation she is dealing with now is very low blood pressure and a heart rate that is elevated. They had to get two new IV locations tonight, which was difficult but finally got things in place. She is being given three different IV antibiotics because of possible infection and IV fluids because of her fluid level being so low. Please pray tonight that tomorrow will be good for Natalie, and she will be feeling better soon. Thanks, Sandy. (October 10th 2007)" When mom finished reading she asked if it sounded ok and if I wanted her to post what she had written. So many people had been lifting my name up in prayer, and they all had helped so much. People read the post and all the post before and left such encouraging words.

In the ICU it is always daytime, I believe. Every hour you have a nurse coming in to check on you, give you more medicine or see how you are. I wasn't getting a lot of sleep, but I felt some improvements. My mom and I both had to agree that it's amazing how the days and nights tend to run together after awhile. The morning came, and my mom and I were both wide-awake. I felt stronger today, but they still would not allow me to get out of bed for any reason. Even though I may have felt some better, I had a long road ahead.

We were just sitting there talking as my mom began to brush my hair. She was just talking away. All I could say was "STOP!" She stopped and asked what was wrong. I said, "My hair is falling out"! She looked at the brush, and the brush was filled with my beautiful brown hair. My mom had to clean out the brush a few times and then get the hair off of the back of my gown. I told myself I was okay with it, but I knew I really wasn't. I knew it was going to happen, but I just didn't know when. I wasn't ready to think about losing my hair right now with so much else going on that was out of my control. We stopped, and I put my hair in a bun. That was all I could handle.

My mom had gone down to the 1st floor just to get out of the room for a bit, but I was okay because my dad was in the room with me. He was sitting in a chair close to my bed working on things for work. The TV was on, but neither of us was paying much attention to it. The brush my mom had used was lying at the end of my bed. I took my hair back down, picked up the brush and pulled the trashcan close to my bed. I began brushing my beautiful hair into the trashcan. I could see out of the corner of my eye, my dad looking at me with a sad look on his face. It broke my heart because I knew it was hard for him to sit there and watch his little girl do that. My eyes burned as I could feel the tears building up and begin to run down my cheeks. I don't know why I was brushing my hair out but the faster it comes out, the faster it would grow back.

I was angry. Wasn't this perfect? Now my hair was falling out? I wanted to throw that brush at the wall and never see it again. I knew this was going to happen, but you can't ever prepare yourself. The entire unknown was hard to deal with, but it was also hard to accept the fact that I was going to look like a cancer patient. I was still new to this whole cancer deal, so I wanted to deal with it a little at a time. I wanted to throw my hands up, look up and yell, God, you win. I couldn't fight against His plan for me. Physically I was so weak, and now mentally and emotionally my world was crumbling down. What was next? Would I wake up the next day and be bald? How about next week? I didn't know, and nobody could answer that. All I ever heard was each person is different. I just wanted to know what was ahead, and nobody could tell me, nobody.

I looked up and saw my mom through the glass sliding doors of my room. I was happy my mom and dad were both there now. They brought warmth to that cold hospital room.

The day grew longer when one of my IVs stopped working and had to be discontinued. I think my veins were finally giving up too. Later that day the only IV left stopped working as well. I had to have an IV by 6:00 p.m. to keep my antibiotics and other meds on schedule.

My mom received a phone call asking what all had been going on. Mom stepped outside of the Unit to talk on her phone because she didn't want to upset me when people would call by talking about how I was doing. It was hard to have to deal with everything that was going on, but it made it even harder to have to listen to the same things over and over when people called. Mom asked the lady on the other end of the line just to pray they could start another IV and get it started on the first try.

About that time the doctor walked in and said he had to get things moving. My stomach felt like it had completely turned upside down and I couldn't speak. I was tired of being poked and just wanted everyone to leave me alone. By the time everyone got in my room, I think we had every nurse along with the doctor in my room trying just to find one vein, just one!

An older nurse everyone called Grandma sat at the end of my bed and prayed aloud. They all knew what a hard day and night before it had been for me due to IV issues. I was running out of places to put an IV. It was like finding a needle in a haystack. My hands looked so fragile from all the previous needle sticks, and my arms looked like I had been beaten up due to the blood thinner I was on. It was impossible to find a vein through the black, blue, and yellow colors that looked painted on my arms. The only words I could hear from one of the nurses were "okay honey here we go", and I held my breath until they said they had gotten it. Patients get used to being stuck like a pushpin, and I was fine with it, but my body was consumed with pain and exhaustion. God had answered another prayer and proved that everything was in his control. I felt like maybe God was finally stepping in and seeing that I could barely take much more.

The evening settled down and by now only one nurse was coming in my room for the rest of the night. That night mom and I decided to do something besides just sit there. The Child Life Specialist had come by earlier and left some stuff for me to do if I felt like it. This week at the hospital the theme was All About Me, and patients were given a canvas to glue pictures, quotes, words or anything that described them on the board. That is what mom and I worked on. Mom's chair stayed next to my bed, and we cut out letters to spell out my name, quotes, pictures, and things that described me. It was nice to fill the room with the smell of glue instead of alcohol pads, laughs instead of tears, laughter instead of voices.

I felt sick, but I always felt awful, and I wanted to do this. I wanted for both my mom and me to do this. I needed this. I looked at the board and saw all these things that were bigger than cancer and that cancer couldn't take away from me. Cancer might have distanced me from a lot of the fun things in my life, but this monster would never take these things away me. The fun lasted as long as it could, and I could barely hold my eyes open any longer. Mom continued to sit right beside me. Several times during the week I would wake up in the middle of the night and see my mom sitting in that uncomfortable chair sleeping. Even for a few seconds, I thought about how blessed I truly am to have such a great family, especially parents. My parents were there and would be there for me no matter what I had to go through. I know it has to be hard on them to see their daughter go through something that no one has any control over, not even me. My dad had left a comment on my Caring Bridge page, and that was the most important one anyone could ever leave me. This is what he wrote me:

Good Morning Sweetheart,

Seventeen years ago, I stood over your bed and prayed "Lord, please strengthen her little body and bless the doctors and nurses tending to her so we can take her home." This morning, my prayer is the same. Yet, the thought and feelings are so much more. I love you more than I could ever have imagined 17 years ago. I am so proud of you. I am so thankful the Lord answered my prayer and made you into the wonderful young lady for everyone to love and enjoy. Your sweet personality, kind heart, love for people, cute laugh, neat sense of humor, tremendous creativity, beautiful smile, amazing one-liners, positive attitude, and faith in God has been a blessing to all. I believe God will answer our prayers again today! Be strong, keep your positive attitude and keep working that sense of humor. :-) I love you!

Love, Daddy

My dad always knows how to make me smile. God did have a plan for me, and I was starting to see that. Having prayers being answered these past few nights made my faith grow stronger. God was working right in front of my eyes.

Another busy day was ahead of me; the doctors had scheduled a few more things than earlier in the week. First, I had to get a CT scan done to make sure everything was still okay, or rather not any worse, but nothing was just okay. Later during the day, I would have my PICC line put in my right arm. Getting my PICC line back in was going to be great because I knew it would allow them to use that for blood work and any more IV meds I might need. I was actually excited about this…who was I?! I was still worried, but after the week I had been having nothing was surprising me anymore. The doctor explained that being on the blood thinner shots it would be almost impossible to get another blood clot, so that put my mind at ease about having to go through all of this again. Since today was only the first day my blood pressure was staying at a safe level and they wanted it to stay that way, they decided to take me down for my CT scan in my bed. I felt like I was being paraded down the hall in my bed. I probably even scared some kids because I looked so awful.

Chapter 7

Under Lock Down

While in ICU, I wasn't able to get out of bed at all. When my nurse and mom told me I wasn't able to get out of bed, I looked at them like they were crazy, and they quickly told me they weren't with big smiles on their faces. I didn't like laying in bed all day and not being able to get up, but that didn't matter. I didn't want to go run laps around the hallways, but was getting up and going to the bathroom such a big deal? To them it was, and that's when the nurse smiled again as she held up, what I like to call, "Betty the Bedpan". This is for sure not something to joke about with anyone, but especially a 17-year-old girl, and let me tell you they were not joking. If you have experienced this you know the weird and awkwardness of this process, if not, then consider yourself lucky.

I told my nurse and mom many times that I was fine and I could get up and could just walk to the bathroom. I truly wanted to believe that I could, but the second I would try and get up I would come right back down. I felt so bad that I just gave in. I was fully capable of taking care of myself before, and now I had to use a bedpan. Could this get any more embarrassing? Mom knew I hated all of this, but she would always try to make me feel better and say I could put this in my book. My response was always just rolling my eyes. The nurse came in and got me ready to get my PICC line back in. We went down to the room where my other line was put in and talked with the doctor that was going to be putting it back in. All I could say was, "I'm back." I had my blanket, and I was ready to get this thing back in. The stress and worries in the room seemed to be at ease this time. I'm not sure if it was all the pain medicine I was on or if it was the nurses that were making me laugh so much. I hadn't laughed in so long, and here I was laying on the table not wanting to get put to sleep because we were all laughing. I was always treated so well at St. Jude, but in that operating room I was being treated like a 17-year-old, and talked to like a real person. It was great.

I woke up to a nurse pushing my bed back to my room. Before I even made it back to the room, I was asleep. My parents weren't up there at the time, but I knew they would find their way back to me. I guess after spending the week in the Unit I didn't panic as much this time when I realized my parents right there with me when I got back. Later, I woke up, and my parents were in my room peacefully waiting for me to wake up. They told me that had been sitting downstairs waiting for me and didn't know I was already in my room.

The nurses had seen my parents after taking me back to my room and told them I was done. That night I had a nurse we hadn't seen all week, and it's hard to get a new nurse when you get used to the one you've had the past few days. She was friendly, and I didn't mind her. Mom told me later that she made her nervous, and I guess I just hadn't paid any attention. At one point during the night, my blood pressure started dropping again. My nurse got really nervous and decided to go ahead and start me back on Dopamine. My mom had been watching my blood pressure the past few days, and although it was low, she didn't think I needed to be put back on such a powerful drug. My mom didn't say much and just let the nurse do her job. After the nurse started the medicine and left the room, I started feeling really weird. My heart began racing, and my head was pounding. I didn't know what was happening, but it was not okay. My mom instantly stepped outside the room to tell the nurse something wasn't right. Mom spoke up and said I didn't have this type of reaction the first time the medicine was given to me and was very concerned as to what was happening. The nurse told us she couldn't stop the medication without the doctor's orders, but she could pause it. My mom wasn't sure what to do. She didn't want her to pause it, and it put me in danger, but she didn't want me to keep feeling like that. It was causing my heart rate to elevate even more, the pounding in my head wouldn't stop, and my chest was now hurting. This wasn't right, and mom told her to pause the medicine. As soon as the Dopamine was stopped my hearted stopped racing, head stopped pounding, and chest pains weren't as bad. Right then we all knew the right decision was made. She didn't have the medical training that the nurse had, but she had been with me all week, and it is amazing what you learn and know by the time you are put through stressful situations in the Unit.

All that excitement finally ended, and I was very ready to get some rest. The next morning one of my doctors came to see how I was doing and thought it would be best to put me on a regular floor. My mom did tell the doctor about what happened the night before, and my doctor said I needed to be moved before something else happened. She told me I would able to rest a lot more on a regular floor, but I still needed to be monitored.

Bridget was my nurse today, and she was awesome. She pulled up a chair and sat and talked to me for a long time. It was mid-morning, and I was feeling a lot better. I was ready and needed to take a shower though. Bridget said they had a waterless shampoo I could use, but I wanted the real thing! I did, however, try the waterless shampoo, and it was a joke. Thank goodness for the Grandma nurse that had been with me during the week, she thought I'd be okay and that it might be good for me to get out of bed and get a warm shower. I was so glad to hear this because I had been flat in bed for a week. My mom got the press-n-seal, Bridget got the towels and wheelchair, and I sat there like a little kid with a huge smile on my face.

I rode in the wheelchair down the hall to the shower. I got in the shower, and then Bridget and mom made sure I was doing okay. They didn't want me to pass out, so they had to help out. That shower was great! Then when I started washing my hair, it started falling out. Even though my hair had been falling out earlier during the week, it was falling out a lot more when I washed it. As I handed the shampoo bottle outside of the shower curtain to my mom, she asked if I was ready for conditioner. I couldn't even speak through the tears that were falling down my face. Finally, I somehow said yes, and right then everyone was worried and kept asking what was wrong. In more of an angry tone, this time, I said my hair was falling out. They tried to convince me that it was all right, but it wasn't, because what part of being bald was going to be all right?

I knew my hair was going to fall out, but it was just the shock of seeing it lying at my feet instead of it on my head. My hair was one of the things I loved about myself, and I couldn't think I could ever live without it. I wasn't going to have a choice though. I didn't know if I was going to end up losing all of my hair that day, the next week, in a few months, or even at all. Every story I heard about patients losing their hair was different. My shower ended, and I headed back to my room. The hot shower was fantastic but almost too much. I stayed in bed the rest of the afternoon while Bridget sat in there with mom and me. I was Bridget's only patient, so it was great to have her hang out. I wanted to curl up in a ball and never move. Bridget and mom could tell I was upset, so she decided to paint my nails for me. I needed to feel pretty in some way, and that helped, but it didn't take away the feeling I had about my hair.

Later we got my things ready and finally got to move into a regular room. I was so excited! I was still on high-powered antibiotics and would be on them for the next few weeks. I would still be monitored a lot on the 2nd floor, but not as often so I could at least get some sleep. On the way down to my new room I had to wear a mask, I looked like a ninja turtle. Wearing it for the first time you feel like everyone, and their mom is looking at you, but you then realize you look like the other patients. The hospital was calm and quiet, and not a whole lot going on. There weren't that many people out and about because it was already late Friday afternoon and most appointments were over. As my parents, nurse, and I were almost to my room I passed a little boy sitting in a wagon wearing a mask too. He was a lot cuter than me.

When we returned to my room, we just talked and watched TN. I liked just sitting there with my dad, and we didn't even have to talk just his presence made me feel better. When mom got back to the hospital, my dad headed back home. Around 9:00 that night my brother James and his girlfriend, Angela, showed up, and mom went to meet them at the front of the hospital. Wow, it was so encouraging to see them. They were tired from working all day, but they wanted to visit. They stayed for a little while, and that's all I not only wanted but also needed. We sat and talked for a while and then got the wheelchair and showed them around the hospital. They headed back to Henderson soon after that and mom and I headed back to the room.

On our way back we decided to pick up a movie from the area they have entertainment for patients. We decided on Pretty Woman because I had never seen it, and had heard it was good. We only got through about half of the movie, and I was ready for bed. It had been a busier day, and some good sleep was exactly what I needed. The nurse came in a few times during the night, but not as many as previously. One time during the night the nurse came in and took my blood pressure, and I didn't feel right. When I stood up I could already tell if I didn't sit down I was going to pass out again. The nurse helped me sit down and then took it. My blood pressure was lower, but it was still in a safe range. I got some rest that night and felt a little better the next day.

The doctor that had been seeing me during the week came in to see how I was doing later that morning. He told me that I could go home today! I was so excited and couldn't believe it! Since I was going to be on antibiotics for the next few weeks, the nurse was going to have to show mom how to hook up my PICC line to them. It didn't seem like it would be hard, but we wanted to make sure we knew what to do. They had to be put in the refrigerator and were in this unusual vacuum-packed container. This was just one more thing for my mom to have to learn so she could take care of me. I rested the majority of the day while everyone worked on getting our bags together. After I was discharged, the nurse got a wheelchair and instructed to wear my mask again out to the car and when I got home because of so many germs. Bridget had heard I was going to be sent home, so she came down to help us get all of our stuff together and into the car. She was such an excellent nurse and huge help to mom and me.

Home was our destination! I would never have thought that just riding in a car would make me feel ill or tired, but it did. I had a great welcoming home team when I got home, and I was so happy. I wish I could have felt better after walking through the door, but I didn't and knew it was going to be like this for a while before I did. I went to my room, didn't worry about making sure everything was off my bed I just laid down. My grandma and Aunt later showed up to see me. It was great to see them. They sat on my floor, and grandma just gave me the biggest hug you could ever imagine. With tears in her eyes, I could see how worried she had been about me. It hurt to see everyone cry, but I didn't know how to help so I just cried too.

As the night went on I began to feel worse and worse. My body had an ache that never seemed to go away. The only thing to help make me feel at ease was my pain medicine and after taking that I always fell asleep. It had been a long day, but honestly what day hadn't been long? Mom had wondered if we came home too early, but home was where I wanted to be. I didn't have to listen to beeping monitors or have someone wake me up, and so my opinion about coming home was it could have never been too soon.

Chapter 8

Hope for Healing

I knew it was going to take me awhile to get to feeling 100% better, but that wasn't fast enough for me. It didn't seem like anything about this whole thing was passing by fast enough at all. The next day was Tuesday, and it had been the best day I had all week long. My mom even told me I woke up and just looked better. I thought that I always looked good though, right? Feeling a little better was encouraging to me, it reminded me that some days will be okay and better than the bad ones.

My good mood maybe had something to do with the night before. For the first time in awhile, I had been the happiest person. I got to see the puppy I was getting. A family I am close with had Chihuahua puppies and offered to give one to me. They brought one over, and I fell in love. A white with brown spots Chihuahua fit right into my hand. Her nails had been painted pink, and a bow had been tied around her neck. She already had my heart. I sat on the couch as she walked around the floor sniffing everything. When that three-pound puppy was around, the sadness that had wrapped around my heart had let go even if it was just for a little while. I hadn't smiled that big or felt that much happiness in what seemed like ages. Happiness was a familiar feeling; it had just been a very distant thing in my life for a long while. Having this puppy meant I would have company when everyone else was at school or work. She would keep me moving instead of lying on the couch the whole time. Although the thought of how I would take care of her when I could barely take care of myself did cross my mind more often than not. Even when talking with my parents about getting a dog they couldn't say no…I mean I had cancer, no one could say no, right? Mom and dad thought I was funny, but in all seriousness, they thought it would be good for me, and realized how much my spirits had been lifted.

As soon as I saw my puppy I knew I wanted to name her Hope. Her name had to mean something and hold importance. Everything in my life whether at St. Jude, home, or anywhere else held hope. We all hope to get better, hope gets us through the day, no one can ever take hope away from us, and now I had a dog that brought hope into my life. I had cancer and this dog was going to be there with me through it all. Would she know that I was very sick and know the reason why I got her? Probably not, but it made me happy.

The next few days I had my ups and downs. What did that even mean though? Sometimes I was getting sick and other times I was actually walking around the house; those were definitely my ups and downs. Mom did decide to take a leave from work for the next 4 months until I was done with treatment. I was really glad she decided to do that because it helped having someone else at home while I was sick. Mom said seeing me so sick scared her, and she didn't want to have to go through that again so staying home was the only option.

Halloween was coming up and I was planning on carving pumpkins. I might be sick, but I still wanted to enjoy my life. I didn't always feel good, but I didn't always feel bad either. There were rough days, but good days so I wanted to enjoy what I could. Spending time with my family was important to me. The only outings we did were going to St. Jude and that wasn't that much fun...if any. We grew closer to each other not only because it was such a hard time, but because we wanted to. I didn't focus on the fact that I could get really sick and possibly not make it, because although that was unlikely, it could still happen. I drew close to the people that I loved, and tried to embrace the good with the bad. I have to say I was better about embracing the good, and not so much with the bad.

The third treatment was a lot better, because I got to come home right after I was done with treatment and didn't have to stay a week like the two previous visits. Getting home this time was a lot better. Hope greeted me at the door like she hadn't seen me in weeks. That made coming back even more enjoyable. I laid down on the couch and Hope stayed right there beside me. Maybe she could make after treatments a lot better for me now.

When the doctor first told me the side affects of taking steroids I just kind of listened, but now that I've been on them awhile I truly understand them. Some of the side affects make my bones hurt so much I start to think I'm turning into an old woman. I honestly tried not to complain to anyone because it didn't help make anything better, but these drugs were making me nervous, pissed off, and sleepless. I promise, no one wants to live with a nervous pissed off cancer kid that hasn't had any sleep. It was weird to me that I just started noticing these things, but it was taking my body that long to get used to them and then decide not to cooperate. This was just my luck, but mom was definitely going to see if we could do anything about these things; for everyone's safety.

The way my steroids worked was 2 weeks on and 2 weeks off the medicine, and these were the two weeks I was on them. No sleep had been in my daily plans and I had more energy than usual. I had stayed up all night sitting in my room. I crocheted for way too long, and all mom could do was laugh. I wanted to go to school, and with no sleep, why not? Mom didn't care as long as I only did what I could, even if that meant talking to people in the halls for just a few minutes and then having to leave. She knew I needed to see other things and people. I got ready and only lasted 30 minutes, but it was a good 30 minutes. I saw people I hadn't seen since I left school, and if anything else showed people that I was alive and kicking as long as I could. I couldn't be involved in school activities anymore, but I still got to be in pictures for the yearbook and sit in the car and watch a football game from the car. Every high school student's dreams, right? It wasn't my favorite thing to do, but I still got to be somewhat involved. It wasn't fair, but life isn't fair, always hit me right in the face once I had those thoughts. I was trying to accept being happy, living the life I had to live now, but when you see others working, going to school, hanging out, you think about how much you are missing out on. It is discouraging, and it sucks.

My whole life revolved around being careful, germfree, medicine schedule, flushing my PICC line, and feeling like there was a green tint to my face at all times. I was happy others got to enjoy their life, I wouldn't want anyone to have to go through this, but sometimes I felt perfectly fine about not being happy for them. Did that make me a bad person? I didn't care, but I don't think it did.

My friends were as busy with their lives as I was with mine. It felt like we lived in different worlds. I didn't know if these things would change, and I couldn't always wonder about it. Some friends were there and some friends were not. When others didn't know what cancer was like or why things had to change I couldn't expect them to understand or stick around. Maybe my healing was going to have to come from myself, and not looking for other people to help me. Maybe I was looking for the wrong people to help with all the healing. Maybe God was just waiting for me to actually look to him for the healing that I really needed. Healing was happening in some way all the time, it was just harder to see it sometimes.

Chapter 9

Accepting Change

The weekend was finally here which meant that my 4th treatment was coming up. I wasn't excited; it's chemo, why would I be excited? The cancer life had become a routine I would never forget. Being home sick, tired, and just lying on the couch was my daily life. I had accepted it. You can't move forward without accepting hard things, and picking yourself up and moving forward.

There are always going to be hard days with or without cancer, but it is important to find the strength to beat those hard days. God was in control even when I doubted that or couldn't accept that. People accept different types of things in their lives all the time, surely it was the time I accepted all of this and tried to move on. The doctors and nurses were in control of the medical side of my life, but even then God was still in control. Letting go of the worry, fear, and a lot of times bitterness wasn't easy to do. It would be a struggle every single day. There is no five-step process, but just finding it within you to put your doubts, fears, and whole life into God's hands helps. I had a sense of relief when I prayed about these things and tried to accept that no matter what happened, things would be okay. I didn't know how everything could be okay, but I was getting there. God had a plan that I apparently couldn't figure out, but it was there. The one thing that was still bothering me was being so lonely. I had an amazing family that surrounded me, but I wanted my friends back. I was sick of not getting to see people. I knew or, at least, felt like it was my fault. I couldn't get out, and I didn't expect people to come see me. I didn't know that my friendships would change so much. At the time, I felt like they weren't even there. I didn't want them to center their life around me, but just hearing from them would be nice. Everyone at the hospital had told me it wasn't unusual for teenagers to back away from people when things like this happen. It is hard for everyone, I understood that, but really, I was the sick one! I wanted to accept my changing friendships, but wished and prayed things would change.

Another week, another treatment, another doctors visit. After finishing with the run down of Dr. Howard's questions, he looked in my ears and throat. I had now developed what was called thrush in my throat. He asked if my throat had been hurting, and it had been but not extremely bad. It was hard to tell the different between new pain and the usual pain. I didn't have a clue what that was, but I knew I would be getting a prescription. He explained to me that thrush happens when you don't have an immune system and a combination of taking chemo drugs, antibiotics, and prednisone. He said I would take something just for a few days and then it should clear up.

We went to the medicine room, and all I needed was chemo. Being hooked up to an IV pole can be very a tricky thing when you have to pee during chemo. The bathroom wasn't very far away, but when you have tubes that you are trying not to trip over and a huge poll you have to drag along with you, it can get interesting. At least, the trip to the bathroom can take up most of the time getting chemo. By the time chemo is over, I am already feeling terrible. It never helps when we walk out the doors and remember that mom parked the farthest from the hospital either. When we made it to the car, I crashed in the backseat. Sometimes you just have to cry because you can't find the words to say how you feel or to make things better. I cried most of the way home. Feeling positive was so easy when I felt good. On the other hand, feeling terrible made it so easy to get discouraged and forget about all the times you promised yourself to think positive or look to God.

We were almost home when I noticed that my nose was bleeding. I had never had a nosebleed. This was a new side effect that completely caught me off guard. Mom realized it was from the blood thinner shots, and that made a lot more sense. The shots may be preventing me from getting blood clots but now, and it was possible I was going to be having other problems because of the shots.

That night was terrible because in addition to the nosebleeds, I was having extremely painful headaches. I have had plenty of headaches before, but this was the kind where the light made it worse, and I couldn't open my eyes. Mom thought it was because I wasn't on the steroids and my body was so used to being on them at such a high dose and now I wasn't on them at all. I figured things would get better after a few days passed. Half way through the week, things were the same if not worse. I was so sick, and nothing helped. There weren't enough wet cloths or trashcans to put by the couch to make things any better. Mom would ask if there was anything she could do, but all I could say was no. Not unless someone had another body of mine lying around somewhere that I didn't know about. How sick did I have to be to actually start feeling like I was getting better?

Hope laid right there with me all during the day. Maybe she knew I was sick and just wanted to be right here? Probably not, but that made me feel good to think that. Another day passed and mom called St. Jude to talk to Wren, my nurse practitioner, and she thought it was best that I come back to St. Jude for them to make sure things were okay. I packed some stuff just in case I would have to stay, but mom figured they would just send us back home. After getting to the hospital, they sent me straight to the clinic. My nurse saw me and instantly knew something was wrong. They started me on IV fluids, Morphine, and a nausea medicine over a period of 4 hours. They said that from the chemo treatments I had developed what is called Esophagitis. This is caused when the drugs/medications break down the lining of the esophagus, and it is very painful. They sent me to the medicine room where I was put in an isolation room. Although, I was in a great deal of pain it wasn't too long and we could tell that the Morphine was making me extremely sick to my stomach. It lessened the pain, but throwing up caused so many other problems. Mom had gone to the cafeteria to grab something to eat, and I was alone in my room. I didn't mind being alone, but I just sat and cried. Mom got back and we both shared tears. We were drained from the inside out.

My meds ended, and we had to stay at the Grizzly House for the night because I had to go back to the clinic the next day. We made it the lobby of the Grizzle House and sat down at the tables. It didn't take long until I was throwing up everywhere. I could have died from being so embarrassed, but when you are that sick, you can't help it. The people there were so nice about it. Mom had to get me upstairs before I got sick anywhere else. I laid on the bed and mom remembered I was the only one to pack a bag. In the midst of all the things that were going on we both laughed. All mom had were the clothes she was wearing, and I had brought some more clothes for me. I knew that from the time I started coming to St. Jude that when I go for something I never just stay one day, and I would rather have clothes and be prepared to stay than end up like what my mom did and not bring anything. We somehow figured something out and went to bed. The next day we both thought I would get looked at by Dr. Howard and then head home, wrong again. Back to the medicine room for another round of fluids, pain, and nausea medicine, maybe, this time would be better, and then I could go back home. My bed was definitely more comfortable than a hospital bed. If I was going to be sick and in pain, I would rather have to deal with it in the comfort of my home, but somehow that never works out.

Chapter 10

Running for a Reason

The time was getting closer when Nicole would be running the 5K in the St. Jude Marathon. I remember the night we found out I was sick. Nicole said that she was going to run in the marathon. At the time, she thought there was a 13-mile and a 26-mile, but that didn't matter to her. Yeah, she wasn't sure how she would ever run 13 miles, but she wanted to do that for me. She then found out there was a 5K, which made being able to participate a lot easier.

Nicole knew that she couldn't take my cancer away, but she could run for me and all the other kids at St. Jude. When Nicole told me she was going to do this for me, it meant everything to me. She knew that she wasn't making a difference by physically running, but by raising money, she knew that would help make it one step closer to help pay for my treatments, help another child, and even one dollar closer to finding a cure against this monster.

Mr. Rich had been running the full Marathon at St. Jude for quite awhile, but this year held even more meaning. He worked at the same University as my dad and another child's dad that was also being treated at St. Jude.

There was usually a large group of faculty, staff, and students that participated as well as raised money. This year people in our town and college could help two people that were being affected by cancer and treated at such an important and wonderful place. T-shirts were sold to help raise money, and I saw how much people wanted to help even with donating a few dollars.

This race was beyond running to cross a finish line. This marathon was about bringing awareness to childhood cancer. This marathon was about raising money to help run a hospital that saves lives day after day. This marathon was about giving hope to families that were experiencing cancer, honoring those who fought their hardest, and celebrating those who survived. This celebration and remembrance event was much bigger than I could ever imagine.

Chapter 11

Thankful for the
Little Things

Thanksgiving day had arrived. I was sick, but I was still alive; that to me was something huge, and for that I was thankful. I was also thankful to be surrounded by family that loved me and was truly taking great care of me. My health wasn't good, I couldn't enjoy all the food that had been fixed, and I had to rest most of the day, but I was with the people I loved. It was easy to forget about being thankful in such a terrible time for us, but couldn't think like that. It made me happy to still see all the good things God had blessed me with even if things weren't going the way I wanted them to. I had cancer, but there was a treatment to make me better. I couldn't be at school with all my friends, but I still could see them. I was at home 24/7, but I had the best mom in the world taking care of me. I wasn't getting to do things healthy teenagers were able to do, but I had a sister that wanted to make each day a little brighter. I wasn't getting the prayer of not having cancer answered, but I was getting smaller prayers answered every day. I couldn't feel myself getting better, but I could feel God easing a lot of the fears I had. Just because things weren't always happy or great, I still had so many things to be thankful for.

I woke up feeling okay. Knots filled my stomach because I knew at some point during the day the phone would be ringing to let us know if I would have to have radiation or not. Once I got up and started moving around the house, I realized I didn't feel as well as I had thought. Hope stuck right by my feet as I went from the bathroom to the couch. She never left my side. Mom, dad, and Angela were going to lunch and asked me to go. I didn't want to but managed to pull myself together enough to go. I wanted to keep my mind busy instead of constantly thinking about the news we were waiting on. All that I could think about was the last time we were waiting for a doctor to call about news. That was when I was just finding out about the cancer. Phone calls from doctors hadn't really worked out in my favor.

When we returned home, there was a message from my doctor to call my clinic back. As my mom stood behind the recliner in the living room dialing the number to my clinic, I sat on the couch. Instantly, I felt hot and had a nauseous wave hit me at once. I didn't know if I should prepare to cry or smile. It was hard to understand what was being said on the phone. Mom had a serious look on her face but gently shook her head no at me. No radiation, no being gone for a lengthy period of time, no leaving Hope at home, but what? They had told me all Hodgkin's patients always had radiation. How could I be such a different patient? They explained to mom that my cancer had responded well to the chemo that the risks of other side effects were greater to receive radiation if I didn't need to than to not receive radiation. That was great news, but I was still waiting for that huge relief feeling to happen. I was glad I wouldn't have to go through more stuff, but I wasn't exactly out of the woods yet.

We sent out text messages to my brother and sister. They had ben waiting to hear the news, and I figured others would find out soon after they knew. In all this excitement that I felt I still wanted to look up and say, God, I still feel alone, and uncertain that this is how things are going to go. It was easy to doubt good news because it seemed like every time we took a step forward with something good; we took two steps back the next day. God had answered such a huge prayer for me; I should have felt his presence and not alone, right? Maybe that feeling of him being near would come back after I had time to process everything. I felt guilty for still having questions and feeling uncertainty, but God and the doctors knew what they were doing. It was just allowing myself to let go of my uncertainty and truly have the faith that I had told myself all along that I had been having.

I was keeping up with my schoolwork the best I could, even if I didn't have much to do. I couldn't focus or hardly read anymore without my head hurting. I hadn't learned anything to do with this years school work anyway. Having an afternoon to myself was nice, and the thought of getting work done was nice, but I couldn't. I would try so hard, but it felt like a loss cause. Not having to do school work might sound great, but when you feel worthless because you can barely take care of yourself and then on top of that you can't even help yourself learn any new school material because your brain is mush. It is a feeling of just taking up space in the world.

I decided to shower, hoping that would make me feel better. Having alone time was great, but it had a lot of disadvantages as well. Wrapping my arm to cover my PICC was a task alone. It's frustrating not even being able to enjoy a simple day at home by myself without needing some damn help.

After managing to waste several strips of tape and more press-n-seal than we should talk about I got my arm covered. I was going to do something for myself if it took me all day long. However, I didn't have all day because a lady from the local paper was coming over to interview me. I never realized how popular a teenager with cancer could be! I didn't mind the questions, and I didn't mind telling my story. I truly did want my story to reach someone that was going through the same thing. If they felt alone and found the story I wanted them to know that I had felt alone too, but I was still fighting each day good or bad with the hope of putting this monster to rest.

The interview went well, and the lady was really nice. Mom filled the lady in on events that had happened; events that seemed so far away to me. Listening to mom talk about different things made it seem like she was talking about someone else and I was just listening to a story. I didn't remember all the things that had happened or maybe my memory seemed fuzzy; it felt like I was living in two different worlds listening to things I remembered and then hearing things that seemed like a dream I just had.

It is difficult to let a stranger inside your world of sickness. I realized that to help someone else out I had needed to let others in, to get my story out there. The table that was covered with medicine bottles, medical supplies, and a puke bucket all the sudden became embarrassing, but it caught the lady's eyes before I could help her out the door. I was used to this life, we all were. The lady stood in amazement saying, "so this is the life as a cancer patient." Those words stung as if someone had just opened a fresh alcohol pad without allowing me to brace myself for such a strong chemical smell. She was right, but there was so much more to being a cancer patient than pills, bandages, and things you hope to throw up in instead of on the floor. I guess her amazement caught me off guard, but I allowed her to take a few pictures of the cancer patient's life before she left.

I was now completely drained. A conversation that left me feeling uneasy in my skin, as if I needed any help with that, did go well, and I knew a good story would be told from it, but there was much more to be told. How was I going to reach other cancer patients and let him or her know they weren't alone by just a simple article that showed a family photo and a table covered in my life of sickness? I even questioned how I could help someone else if I were still having rough days, weeks, and at the rate I was going months? I truly didn't have any answers.

Mom, Nicole, and I headed to church that night. I sat in the pew, but my mind was elsewhere. I wasn't trying to turn my back on worshiping God, but my thoughts were jumbled, and crying babies were eating my last nerve for supper. I was ready to get my 2nd shot of the day, walk a lap down our road with mom, and go to bed. My mood swings sucked, and I wanted to be in a good mood, but good moods weren't exactly that easy to find when taking those awful steroids. Sleep was what my body craved the most, and that didn't even want anything to do with me.

Sleep or no sleep, mom was right on schedule at 8:00 a.m. with my medicines. I felt better and thought I might have looked better, but that might have been stretching the truth. I needed that boost for the day even if it was just a small one. I didn't know what the day's plans were, but I had the feeling it would be a good one. Maybe that was God's way of telling me that he was still in control and helping me just the way I needed to be helped. I had to give God the room to work in my life every day to heal me, not just physically, but mentally and emotionally. I needed him to pull me through the dark days, but also through the good days.

Chapter 12

11,000 Strong

Thousands of people come to Memphis every year to be a part of this one big event. Millions of dollars are raised each year to help support the hospital. It made sense to have a huge fundraiser like this; it cost a million dollars to run St. Jude just for one day. I had never put much thought into the race until now. We had been raising money, Nicole had been training, and everyone was getting excited, but I had never thought of how many people would be there. The excitement of the marathon was everywhere, but that did not erase the dread of chemo in a few days as well. The end of treatment was getting closer, but it was hard to get excited about it. Of course, I wanted chemo to be over and done with, but I felt like I couldn't get my hopes up. It seemed too soon to get excited about cancer almost being over. I could not risk any more setbacks at this point.

Wrapping my head around what life would be like without being marked with a patient bracelet, and waiting for a list of daily activities to print was hard to do. It was a nice thinking that I would still be a patient without biohazard bags coming towards me every other week. This weekend was a celebration, as hard as it was to think about celebrating, I did still have a life to celebrate. Thousands of people would be crowding the streets to get exhausted and to cross an imaginary line that revealed if your speed was good, or if you were slow, and of course somewhere in the middle. I had to remind myself that I was not the only patient at St. Jude, and all the people coming for this event were here to celebrate a life or previous life of someone they loved. That was a reason to celebrate. If I wanted to be bitter about my situation, that was fine, but I should still be happy for other people. That, at least, sounded like the right thing to tell myself.

Wake up feeling good, and in no time, that feeling gets shot to hell. Today, I had to get up. I had to shower, and actually look like I cared what I looked like because before we headed to Memphis for the weekend, we were stopping by the high school to get a group picture of everyone in his or her marathon shirts. The shirts had my face on it. I didn't mind a shirt with my face on it at all, it was funny actually, but I was not wearing my own face on a shirt. I felt sick, but that wasn't new, that almost was a feeling that I didn't notice anymore. The feeling that made me want to hibernate was just the nervousness I get when I get around a lot of people. Everyone wants to hug, talk, and see how I'm doing, but I can't do that. I can't carry on a constant conversation with someone without getting out of breath. I can't ignore how tense my whole body gets when someone grabs me to give me a comforting hug. The hugs are painful and awkward because all I can think about is my PICC line sticking out from my arm. I didn't mind being around people, I liked the company, but it just made me nervous. Mom usually went into the school with me, but she ran errands while I went in alone. She was my protector when I wanted to talk to people, or we had a secret look that only she knew when I was ready to leave. I grew to feel like she had to go with me. What 17-year-old feels that way? Me. I wasn't embarrassed by it, I wasn't a regular teenager anymore, I was a teenager with cancer, and this girl just needed her mom.

The morning of the marathon came faster than expected. I didn't sleep well, was already tired, and had not even made it out of bed. It was going to be such a long emotional day. I started getting ready, and I couldn't shake the thought of how many people were there because of one place. There would be some people there running just to complete another marathon, but most people had someone in mind that they were running the marathon for. I wanted everyone participating to know how much it meant to me that they were doing this for a place that had been saving my life. I did not look like a cancer patient. I had hair and plenty of weight on my bones to disguise the cancer. No one could see my bones aching, feel the waves of nausea that never seemed to cease, or having to constantly check the time to see when the next medications would have to be taken. To every set of eyes there, I was one of them, I could get lost in the crowd, and no one would be able to tell that I was one of the reasons it took St. Jude a million dollars to function for a day.

Nicole and mom headed to the starting line while dad and I headed to the finish line seating. People filled AutoZone Park to watch people cross the finish line. Two huge finish lines overpowered the people. A clock hung over the end of each of the finish lines. What a weird and powerful scene that was to me. The clock meant everything to some runners while it meant nothing to others. Personally, the huge digital clock filled me with excitement and a sense of doom. The excitement I felt was for Nicole. As each minute passed, it was a minute closer to seeing her cross that imagery line that meant absolutely nothing to cancer, but everything to the person cancer was living within. The doom of the clock was a feeling of how much time cancer had poisoned me, and as each minute passed, I wonder how much longer it would last. Would I ever really cross the finish line that cancer had me on?

I stood by the finish line until I could barely stand anymore. I spotted Nicole coming into the park, and instantly I became an emotional wreck. Although, it was just running, the whole thing had nothing to do with running a race anymore. My sister had put her whole heart into something just for me. She raised money to help support finding a cure against something she personally could never take away. She crossed the finish line with a smile and ended her run with a silent hug. That moment was untouchable, real, and explained us more than anything else.

Kayla and her family filled the seats behind us, and this was a day that cancer was not winning. Before, the day was over there was one more person I had to see cross the finish line was Mr. Rich. He told me running 26 miles was a lot easier than any person going through cancer. That might be true for some, but this girl could not even run a mile, so I believe chemo might be better for me than 26 miles. His passion for helping St. Jude was contagious. There was not a dry eye in our crowd when he finished. Through tears, he looked for and yelled for me. All we could share at that moment was a hug swallowed in tears. I was not crying tears of sadness, but possibly tears of relief for him that his legs were still functioning, and tears of blessings. I had such great supporters cheering for me to beat cancer. In the midst of a terrible disease, everything seemed right again. For a few minutes, I had forgotten about the nausea, pain, and chemo. Forgetting about the present situation I was in had been the outcome of the weekend. I had escaped, only for a few minutes, but I had escaped the feeling of the monster inside of me.

Chapter 13

Needing Hope

My body was completely exhausted, and it had been a long day. Before heading back to the hospital, I had one stop to make. Mom had asked earlier if I wanted something for dinner, but I nothing ever sounded appetizing anymore, until tonight. I simply said I wanted some peanuts, and mom instantly said we could stop at Target. I went on to say that I wanted specific peanuts, like the ones you have to crack open yourself. I did not know where that specific craving came from, and I had heard that I would get weird cravings at the oddest times, and I guess here mine was. We stopped by Logan's Road House, and mom got me some peanuts. I was one happy cancer girl, and enjoyed them the whole way back to St. Jude as mom and I laughed. What a great weekend it was, but reality settled back in while I checked into the Grizzly House.

My 6th treatment was here, and I was already pissed from gaining more weight from my steroids. All my medications decided to work against me when it came to trying to lose weight, but also with just maintaining my weight. I was frustrated and just embarrassed. I hated gaining weight. I felt huge, and there was nothing I could do to help it. I had cancer, could I not just get a break with the whole weight thing?

Treatment went as good as being poisoned could go. It really was fine, and I even felt better than normal after chemo. I was hoping that was a sign of a good week ahead. I have learned that when I think things will go one way, or I will feel a certain way another, it is usually the complete opposite. I felt sick and wanted to lie around, but that was normal. Those things often lessened by the middle of the week, but it only got worse. Maybe this was how it was supposed to start getting. Treatments and days were getting hard; my positive attitude was dwindling very quickly, and I was more discouraged than ever. Life sucked, but that would be true of anyone's life with cancer.

I could always count on one thing to lift my spirits. That was Hope. I needed her more than anything, and I could always count on her to make me feel better. There was something about her company that made this awful dream slightly better. She didn't care what I looked like, if I lost my hair, or if I was grumpy. She loved me and needed me. She had no idea that I loved and needed her just as much.

Chapter 14

One More to Go

It was getting closer to Christmas, and I still wasn't bald. Having hair was on my Christmas list this year. I don't mean that in an "I just want hair for Christmas and make everyone else feel bad for actually wanting cool things for Christmas" kind of way. The only reason I want hair is because it is freezing outside. It was the wrong season not to have hair! I was still throwing up and felt green the majority of my days, but my head was staying warm, and that my friends, is a cancer gals blessing.

It was here, my 7th treatment! The end was in sight! This time a couple from church, Brad and Kristi, met us at the hospital the morning of my treatment. They wanted to see what St. Jude was like, and I wanted to have pictures and videos of what my life has been like for later in my life if I ever decided to take a trip down memory lane with a detour of cancer. I wouldn't forget about this crazy hell of a rollercoaster, but there is something different about looking at pictures of yourself during a certain time in your life instead of just a mental image.

We walked around the hospital in between my appointments, and while waiting for chemo. It was a rather laid back day. These people were our friends, and to share this type of day with someone was a challenge, but the type of challenge that helps you see how much people truly care. We talked about what it was like walking the halls as a parent and patient, what I wanted other people to learn from my fight against cancer, and just talking about what all St. Jude has done for me.

Throughout the conversations, I got winded, and other times felt embarrassed, but that was because I was letting people into a world a lot of people would never see. It isn't easy talking about a huge obstacle standing in your way, especially, if you have to fight continually through that obstacle. I wasn't sad, or even bitter about telling others about this life. I felt different; I didn't point out that these were the hallways mom held me in while I had a breakdown. I didn't remind them that the doctor they met was the doctor who confirmed I had cancer. It was truly about how my life revolved around medical things, not just work or friends or projects.

There were many things to know about one place, and I wanted to tell them about all the positive times I experienced there. The reality was that throughout the positive attitude, feeling good days, God answering prayers, it all still boiled down to cancer.

I introduced them to the doctor that was saving my life, and then walked through the hallways that tried to make being there easier. When people visit St. Jude for the first time, it can be overwhelming. Visitors walk around in amazement while I basically drag my feet to a scale that tells me how much the steroids have made me gain weight, or the awaiting liquids that are suppose to cure me, but causes me to look like a weird puffy red faced blowfish.

However, it is pretty neat to see someone's face light up when they hear the amazing stories. It is a reminder that even on rough days I am still being treated by one of the most amazing places. On the way home I rejoiced with thoughts of one more treatment! One more seemed easy enough, but I still had to prepare for the storm before I could enjoy the calm.

We had made it to Christmas! I didn't have a list of the things I wanted, and spending time with family truly was the best thing we could ask for this year. However, despite the already sick circumstances and a visit of the stomach bug, everyone had a good Christmas. My grandparents joined us, and it was a recharge for everyone. We spent time together and had the best laughs. You know the ones that make you tear up while doubled over because your stomach hurts so much from laughing. Yeah, those are the best. That was what we all needed. The house felt back to normal with no one in school, at work, or having treatment. We all could easily find many things for which to be thankful. There was a time when I thought I would only feel bitterness towards this awful monster, but over time, I realized some days more than others I was still alive. I still could laugh, had people around me, and along the way found a peace that only I understood, and that I had to learn on my own. Oh, and I still had hair for the time being. I had plenty to be thankful for.

Chapter 15

No Mo Chemo

Tomorrow would be like any other treatment, and I was already tired. Just because this was the last treatment didn't mean it was going to be magical, easy going, and nausea free, although that would be extremely nice.

The next morning, we got up and ate breakfast. We hadn't been sitting there long when in walked my dad. Having both parents there for my last treatment was a great feeling. I wanted everyone to celebrate with me. We sat and waited for the medicine room, and I laid my head on my dad's shoulder. I was tired and hadn't even been awake that long, and having my dad right there was just what I needed. While waiting for my turn, we talked to other patients I had grown to know and love. Seeing the excitement from other patients and families about it being my last treatment was nice, but heartbreaking. However, the thought of never hearing my name called to the medicine room to get that nasty poison caused me to rejoice silently. All good thoughts must be interrupted at some point, and I was being summoned to chemo. For as long as I had heard my name over the intercom, I still never got over the cringe I experienced when it echoed off the walls. Hearing that it is now your turn in the medicine room was like a mild way of saying it was my turn to feel a slight piece of death. Okay, I'm dramatic, but they can't say: your turn to feel like total poop, death for some reason sounds politer, colder, but more polite.

Here it was, my last treatment. My treatment went just like I thought it would. It was over before I knew it. It was incredible how my thoughts and feelings had somewhat stayed the same, but changed a lot too from the first to last chemo treatment. Everyone from my clinic, my parents, Angela, nurses from the medicine room, and even a mom and little girl that had just received chemo as well all stood around me. The nurses began singing a celebration song to me. I didn't know the words, but I knew what it was talking about; their patients had the best smiles and biggest hearts and today I was packing my bags and wouldn't return for chemo anymore. The song ended, and confetti filled the hair. All I could do was cry. My emotions were on overload. I was so extremely happy, but my heart felt so sad. I wanted everyone to have that moment right then, and we all walk out together. I felt bad for celebrating but was still happy. I deserved this happiness. I had made it through chemo. It was hard to celebrate in a place where someone won't ever get to do that. Hugs and pictures filled the last few minutes I was there.

Kim showed up right before I left to remove my PICC line. I was more than ready for that to get out of my arm. The removal was painless and done before I had the chance to think about it. After she was done all I could do was stare at the line. I felt relief for the first time in a long time. I could actually see in plain view something that was out of my body that had been giving me hell.

It was now time to go home. Celebration high would only last so long because chemo would start taking effect. I knew there would be plenty of celebration to come in future.

Chapter 16

Getting on with Life

I was still sick from treatment, but at this point, all I could focus on was this being the last time I would feel like this. It had been months; I could hold out a few more days. Since completing chemo just a few days before I kept thinking after nausea went away things would be back to normal. I wanted to get a head start on these things, and by that I meant, I wanted to go to school.

I had come up with the brilliant plan of being in our school play "The Wizard of Oz", and I was ready to start being a part of that. Not having treatment, or taking, as many pills I thought should instantly make me feel better. I even convinced myself of that and decided I wanted to go to school all day and go to play practice after school. I might have still felt sick, but now I was losing my mind thinking I could do all of these things. I wanted to be a part of all of these things I felt I had missed.

Completing treatment gave me a surge of energy, the kind of energy that makes you feel like you can bounce back and do anything you want to do. My body, immune system, and overall health were far from being back to normal. My body and mind were on two completely different healing schedules. Things had been like that all along, but it took being able to finally see the light at the end of the tunnel for me to realize that. I attended school off and on, but being back at school when I felt well was frustrating. Sitting in a class having to make myself pay attention and work could send me into panic mode faster than biohazard bag of poison.

For months I couldn't read because words seemed jumbled, I couldn't have lengthy conversations because my lungs felt like they were going to give out; now I had to do both of these things at school. More often than not I found myself staring at the teacher, people around me, and even the walls feeling completely lost. I had been taken out of this part of my world, and then just placed back in it. Maybe I wasn't so ready for all of this after all.

Nothing felt right anymore. Conversations were surface, and nothing more than the latest gossip. I didn't care about those things; couldn't anyone see there was more to life than talking about other people? Most nights were spent crying to mom about how bad I hated school, and how different I felt. I wanted to go back to my world of just being at home with her. I never felt out of place at home and didn't ever have to explain myself when I felt terrible. No one seemed to get it, and it was hard for others to understand that I wasn't going to have a body that was completely better and "normal" again for a while.

I wanted to have that familiar feeling of being with friends and walking to class together. Now, it was trying to find words to even say, doing everything I could not to feel awkward, or hoping to get into class and leave without being noticed. Teachers treated me the same, but friends and I were at a loss. A connection that we all once shared had been lost, and I couldn't blame them. Things were different, I was different, but I couldn't help that either.

My friends were there for me, just like I was for them, but it was just a difficult thing.

What do you do when you feel like a stranger? Was I supposed to start all over again with people? Maybe, things were going to fall back into place eventually. I didn't know the answer to any of those questions, but I was willing to give it some time. I couldn't let this type of stress wear my body done. My body and mind had been through plenty; this was supposed to be the healing time for it all. My goal was to focus on each day. All I had to work through was what was happening now. Crying didn't happen every night once mom convinced me that this would all be okay. Things might not end up like I pictured or wanted them to, but that didn't mean things were going to be terrible. I had made it through needles, medicines, blood clots, chemo, bedpans, and thinning hair, some days I felt like I could make it through anything, even tough days at school.

Chapter 17

Trying to be Strong

The dreaded day everyone always told me about was here. I was very confused as to why now, but no one could give me an answer. I dreaded every shower, hairbrush stroke, and going into public. Loose strands turned into handfuls and thinning converted to bald. Why was my hair falling out now? I was done with chemo! Wasn't that the whole reason cancer patients' hair fell out anyway? I was sad, pissed, and beyond embarrassed about what was happening to me. What happened to things getting better? Did I do something wrong, or was I not taking care of myself the way I should have been?

I had been able to dry and straighten the hair I did have, but now my scalp was becoming more visible, and the ends of my hair looked gross. Trying to get ready to leave my house to go anywhere caused a complete meltdown. Mom and I always somehow met in the hallway, and she would wrap her arms around my buried, sobbing face.

No one was ever going to understand why I was losing my hair. I honestly thought people were going to think I was trying to get more attention by cutting all of my hair off. This whole thing was almost over; I did not need one more thing to stir up people talking. Believe me, I could have thought of many other ways to draw attention to myself, without having to still look like a cancer patient. I know hair is just hair, and it will grow back. That wasn't just it for me, though. My hair was something I hadn't completely lost. It hung on with me almost the whole time. It was a security blanket, something to distract from my huge face, and the weight I had gained.

Without skipping a beat mom grabbed her purse, and we were headed out the door to buy hats, bandanas, and scarves. I knew that by the end of the day we would be cutting my hair off, and mom just wanted to make me feel more prepared if I wanted something to cover my head. I wasn't ready to walk around and show off a baldhead. Even though I knew all along this could have happened, I still wasn't ready. You can't prepare yourself for these types of things. You deal with them when they get to you. A lot of people told me they would be proud to walk around baldheaded.

Maybe, but these people had no idea what it was actually like; they were just saying what they think they would do. Until you look in the mirror and do everything you can to cover bald spots, or can no longer even pull your hair up, you do not understand. I can't imagine that anyone would all the sudden be 100% okay with being bald due to a sickness. Advice is nice, but sometimes you have to do things your way and work through it the way that is best for you.

I had been planning on attending the school basketball game that night, but after all of this, there was no way I could show my face in front of that many people. Everyone would stare, and thinking about that made my face red. People had just seen me off and on at school with hair, and now I couldn't even go out because it looked so humiliating. I was terrified to be seen by anyone but my family. Somewhere between lots of crying, comforting words, and yelling, Nicole and a friend, Keely, found a scarf for my head and convinced me to go to the game.

Entering the gym, I could have thrown up, cried, and somehow laughed all at once. We had to walk in front of what felt like a million pair of eyes to sit down. I was right, there were many stares. I held my breath and did an awkwardly swift walk to my seat. Once we sat down with some friends, I could breathe. No one said a word, asked questions or even stared for too long. I even had a friend tell me I looked pretty. Maybe it was sympathy, but I know it was genuine, and it made me feel good whatever the feelings were behind it.

I hadn't died of embarrassment, I had made it through conversations, and nothing awkward was said, and I was okay. Perhaps people were too afraid to say something because of what my response might be, or maybe they didn't know what to say. All of those things were okay with me. At the end of the night, I was so glad to make it through the door and rip that scarf off my head. It was hot, and I was at home for the rest of the night. The night went better than expected. I still wasn't ready for all of this, but it seemed like it was going to be okay.

By the end of the weekend, people should have started calling me patches. Some hair was there, but other places my scalp could be seen without a doubt. It was time. My mom, sister, and aunt surrounded me in the bathroom, and the transformation of my new look began. My sister was rejoicing in the fact that she wouldn't have to clean out hair from the shower anymore. Yes, that is gross, but she understood it was hard on me. My aunt cut my hair pretty short, and it was all even instead of stringy as it had been. I was ready to scalp it, but she and mom thought we just needed to cut it shorter. Why wait if it was all going to fall out anyway? After it was cut, styling my hair started taking place, but I was done. I had sat there as long as I could. To me, the back of my head looked like a duck butt. I wasn't happy and just wanted to be left alone. My hair was still thinning and falling out. It took time for me to actually make eye contact with myself in the mirror. I didn't see myself as beautiful. I just saw a puffy face that was more exposed than ever. I didn't know when I decided that I was only beautiful because of my hair, and now I needed to teach myself to look at the other beautiful things about me.

My hair wasn't going to grow back overnight, or even in a few weeks. After I realized this, and after many tears and frustrating feelings I came to the conclusion to just have fun with it. I got hats, bandannas, and scarfs to match any and every outfit I might have. Whether I was deciding to have fun with being bald or not there were hard days. I didn't wake up feeling beautiful and ready to take on the world every day, and a lot of days I was frustrated. That is a part of this whole journey, being frustrated some days, and completely content on other days. Hair can be a beautiful thing, but is it necessary for me to have to be beautiful? There were many positive things about not having hair…more time to just stand in the shower didn't have hair to fix, getting ready twice as fast. Bald was going to be beautiful to me, and later on, hair would be beautiful to me again as well.

Chapter 18

All Clear

Four weeks had past, and it was time to head back to St. Jude. Dr. Howard wanted to wait that long to let the last treatment completes its job, and then continue with scans, x-rays, and test again. This was the visit that would completely make or break my day.

It was just mom and I again, and walking through the doors having that sterile smell, crying kids, painted walls, IV polls, and sickness hit you in the face like an awkward hug that welcomed me back. I hadn't missed the place itself to be honest, but I missed the familiar feeling of fitting in and not being different. Walking from place to place felt comfortably nice. This place was once a place I completely disliked, but now it was a place of comfort. It was a weird, but peaceful feeling.

IV sticks were now my main problem because I didn't have an easy PICC line. What a small thing to be thankful for these days. What a long day it was going to be. Today was supposed to be painless, just a few scans, seeing the doctor, and hearing good news. I had pictured it that way at least. The morning ended in tears, but with a working IV. The pain wasn't the cause of the tears, but stress that came along with a lot of emotions about the news that would be waiting for me at the end of the day. My iPod was charged and ready for me to escape to somewhere else while having my PET and CT scans. The second part of the day was focused on x-rays, EKG, and seeing Dr. Howard.

The day seemed blurry, and I felt out of touch. My mind was lost in thought, fearing that this might not be the end of my cancer. I thought being gone for a few weeks would make me feel out of place being back, but it didn't. I felt like a cancer patient. I wasn't sure what was supposed to be different, but I thought it would all be different. This visit was stressful, but it did feel like the calm after the storm. Fingers crossed that this was really the calm, and no storms would be after this visit.

Throughout my scans, I wasn't scared, but my body shook from being nervous. I felt like things would be okay, but something in my body still was making me doubt that. I had come so far since that very first scan. I actually now could make it through both without having to pee. That was an accomplishment to say I've come a long way, right?

The only thing left for the day was to meet with Dr. Howard. This wasn't a waiting game any longer. It was good news or bad news, cancer or no cancer. I wanted to know. I needed someone to tell me, now. Dr. Howard, followed by a medical student, came in the room. All of the sudden the room felt much bigger than it was, my heart felt like it was bouncing between my stomach and throat ready to make me throw up at any given second.

All the typical questions were asked, how I was feeling, any knots, lumps or bumps, and what I had been doing since last being seen. While Dr. Howard stepped out of the room to see if the rest of the test results were back, the med student asked about what all I had been through. I had forgotten how much I loved the awkward small talk with the med students. It was always fun to see how big their faces would get when I got to the ICU part of my story. I made light of all of it, but I could tell they didn't know how to act.

Dr. Howard entered the room breaking up the conversation with a smile from ear to ear. With thumbs up, he said, "All clear!" I was cancer free and in remission! Those were the best words a cancer patient can hear. I could feel my mom's smile without even looking at her. We did it! I did it! I beat cancer. Our celebration didn't last long, but just the right amount of time. There would be plenty of celebrating going on after I took a nap. It was home now for a couple of months, and then back for a short check up. I could handle that with no problems.

On the way home, mom and I just kept saying it doesn't feel real. It had not sunk in yet that the monster that once tried to rip my life and body apart had been beaten. We cried and listened to the music of Colbie Caillat. Tears of joy filled my eyes with tears of sadness for other people still suffering filling my heart. Mom had been calling everyone and telling them the good news. I text Nicole, Cliff, and Kayla because I figured between the three of them news would travel the fastest. It had been a good, but extremely tiring day. I looked the same and felt the same. I wasn't sure if I was expecting some big change. I wasn't disappointed, but I felt as if all the pain and memories were supposed to vanish. Life was just continuing, and the past wasn't going to disappear. Picturing what this day would be like was something I had done since September 13th, and now that it was here, the picture was entirely different. My heart was filled with such great happiness, but yet it was still heavier than I ever could imagine. The pain was over but still made the hairs on my neck stand straight up when thinking about the past several months. Would I always feel this way? I wanted to know if there would be a time I could look forward to, of not having a sick feeling about it all.

My feelings felt wrong. I was being pulled in two opposite directions of happiness and bitterness. I was more thankful than I had ever had been. I made it, and cancer was now in my yesterdays instead of tomorrows. I felt sad for being so happy. My mind wandered to all the other people at St. Jude. These feelings were confusing, but it was time to celebrate. The rest of the feelings I had would be dealt with later. We didn't have a big party when I got home because I was so tired. We rejoiced with hugs, and excitement filled the air on its own. We had plenty of time to celebrate, and if it was up to me, we were going to be celebrating every day for the rest of my life.

Going back to school was still a big challenge for me. I couldn't understand why my body still felt sick and rundown. Nausea was still a problem along with catching my breath when talking to people. Heartburn had settled in and happened on a daily basis. I started wondering if my body did not get the memo to get off the crazy roller coaster it had been on because it was still acting this way. I was done with that roller coaster. Even better, I was done with that theme park and ready to never return again. I was at the end of cancer's road and barely recognized myself. I could vividly remember what I looked like before cancer, and when looking in the mirror now, an entirely different looking girl stared back. I had finally seen how much my body had changed over several months. I was bitter, but I was still alive. How could I argue and be bitter with that?

Mom still knew just what to say when I would get discouraged. She reminded me for days at a time that it was going to take several months to get back to feeling normal, but that I would get there. I still had Hope that loved me for me regardless of what cancer was or what it had done to me. I had great things to look forward to in the months ahead, and that was what needed to focus on now.

Any change process isn't always easy. Accepting my life before, during, and after cancer were all different types of changes. There were good and bad, awful and terrible, peaceful and happy, sad and lonely times throughout the last several months.

There was a time when I was always telling people things were fine and that I was staying positive. I felt that if I were strong everyone else would be too. This eventually caught up with me, and I just lied about those feelings. I wanted to always have that positive attitude, but I couldn't. It took awhile for me to realize that I wasn't honest with myself about everything, but it can be easier to pretend things are better than they are. Being in remission was tricky. I kept a lot of feelings inside and never talked about them, and sometimes that works for people. For me, it didn't, and I was left lonely and hurting. I didn't understand these feelings, so how would anyone else? My heart and mind fought against each other with my real emotions for a very long time.

I had to stop looking ahead and see what I wanted things to be like and work through things that were happening now. God hadn't left me and even though I was well, but he didn't feel that close anymore either. Emotions, stress, and celebration somehow had pushed me away from where God was. My life wasn't directly in a storm anymore, and because of that, it was harder for me to have that unshakable faith that I once had. I felt and saw God working in incredible ways throughout being sick, but I needed to allow myself to see those incredible things still working because difficult days were still a constant thing. It doesn't matter what kind of storms our lives might be in; we need that faith every day. Whether it is cancer, feeling lonely, or just having a terrible, horrible, no good, very bad day, we need to still have that strong faith through less difficult times and the more difficult times.

My journey with cancer has been completed, and I have won. I was surrounded by hope on good days and searched for it on rough days. My reason for Hope was simply to help get me through all my cancer days whether good or bad. We did that together. There will always be a battle with worries, memories, scars, and stress that a survivor will face. I can't say if all these emotions will one day go away, become a distant memory, or visit me on a daily basis, but I will deal with those things when they arrive. I can say that I am a survivor and that I never gave up. Whether a survivor, parent, sibling, current patient, family member or friend, everyone has their own story.

This roller coaster of a journey is a small part of my story, and although this part has come to an end, being a survivor will continue.

Natalie Cravens' world was turned upside down when she was diagnosed with cancer at 17. This book tells the story of the ups and downs not only she, but also her family faced. Be prepared to laugh, cry, and experience her journey with cancer as she tells of the days she spent battling being diagnosed, changes, treatments, friends, and learning to cope with a new routine. May you find comfort in knowing there is a reason for hope during life's rollercoasters even if the hope is your dog.

82314462R00059

Made in the USA
Columbia, SC
01 December 2017